Encouraging Diversity in Higher Education

Encouraging Diversity in Higher Education: Supporting Student Success provides an overview of the widening participation movement in higher education in the United Kingdom, United States, Australia and New Zealand. It argues that universities should revitalise their learning and teaching practices to better meet the diverse learning needs of contemporary undergraduate students.

Approachable in execution, this book provides an evidence-based set of classroom practices, which readers will readily be able to relate to and use successfully, answering questions such as:

- How can I enrich my undergraduate teaching?
- How can I help undergraduate students engage fully with their learning?
- How can I help undergraduate students to quickly acclimatise to higher education?
- How can I help undergraduate students from diverse backgrounds excel at university?

This book discusses the economic and discursive drivers used to increase the number of undergraduate students who were the first in their families to enter university, and some of the ways in which universities responded to the growing percentage of such students. In so doing, it considers the learning needs of diverse students, and discusses the views of academic teaching staff who have used transparent pedagogies in their classrooms.

Including forty-five teaching strategies designed to generate highly engaged, socially inclusive classrooms, this is the first book to offer both a theoretical background of the need to approach learning and teaching in contemporary universities in innovative ways, and a practical, step-by-step guide to using a suite of transparent pedagogies. These focus on building inclusive classroom communities, generating academic literacies, developing collaborative learning skills and encouraging students to think critically.

This book will be a useful companion both for early career academics and those with experience but dealing with a new student cohort. It will also be of great interest to those teaching or studying the many professional qualifications in tertiary education.

Kate Hughes is the President of the Australian Sociological Association (TASA) and a consultant in higher education. She has provided advice in higher education policy and practice to universities in Australia, New Zealand and the United States. She is the co-author of *Australian Sociology: A Changing Society*, the market-leading undergraduate text in Australia, now in its fourth edition.

Encouraging Diversity in Higher Education

Supporting student success

Kate Hughes

LONDON AND NEW YORK

First published 2017
by Routledge
2 Park Square, Milton Park, Abingdon, Oxon OX14 4RN

and by Routledge
605 Third Avenue, New York, NY 10017

Routledge is an imprint of the Taylor & Francis Group, an informa business

© 2017 K. Hughes

The right of K. Hughes to be identified as author of this work has been asserted by her in accordance with sections 77 and 78 of the Copyright, Designs and Patents Act 1988.

All rights reserved. No part of this book may be reprinted or reproduced or utilised in any form or by any electronic, mechanical, or other means, now known or hereafter invented, including photocopying and recording, or in any information storage or retrieval system, without permission in writing from the publishers.

Trademark notice: Product or corporate names may be trademarks or registered trademarks, and are used only for identification and explanation without intent to infringe.

British Library Cataloguing in Publication Data
A catalogue record for this book is available from the British Library

Library of Congress Cataloging in Publication Data
Names: Hughes, Kate Pritchard, 1961-
Title: Encouraging diversity in higher education : supporting student success / Kate Hughes.
Description: New York : Routledge, 2017.
Identifiers: LCCN 2016001166 (print) | LCCN 2016013797 (ebook) |
ISBN 9781138899728 (hbk : alk. paper) | ISBN 9781138899735 (pbk : alk. paper) |
ISBN 9781315707679 (ebk)
Subjects: LCSH: Critical pedagogy.
Classification: LCC LC196 .H84 2017 (print) | LCC LC196 (ebook) |
DDC 378.1/982–dc23
LC record available at http://lccn.loc.gov/2016001166

ISBN: 978-1-138-89972-8 (hbk)
ISBN: 978-1-138-89973-5 (pbk)
ISBN: 978-1-315-70767-9 (ebk)

Typeset in Galliard
by Taylor & Francis Books

Contents

List of figures vii
List of tables ix
Acknowledgement xi
Introduction xiii

1 The inclusive university? 1
2 Teaching the taught 19
3 Building a dialogic classroom: names matter 43
4 Improving academic literacies 67
5 Collaboration 93
6 Thinking critically 113
Conclusion 133

Index 135

Figures

2.1	Trends in enrolment rates 2000–2012	20
2.2	University graduation rates 2000–2012	20
3.1	Name tent card template	46
3.2	Example of PowerPoint slide which includes personal imagery	56
5.1	Simple *Socratic Seminar*	104
5.2	*Socratic Seminar* with Research Assistants	105
6.1	Bloom's hierarchy	117
6.2	The Frayer Model	122
6.3	Simple linear model	126
6.4	Topics with sub-topics (or examples) beneath	126
6.5	Topic with sub-topics (or examples) listed to the right	127
6.6	Hierarchical graphic organiser	127
6.7	Hierarchical graphic organiser with multiple parts	128
6.8	Timeline graphic organiser	128
6.9	Sequential graphic organiser	129
6.10	Mind map 1	129
6.11	Mind map 2	129

Tables

3.1	Example of a *People Bingo* sheet	48
3.2	Summary of Stage One, Two and Three community builders	64
4.1	Definitions of commonly used writing prompts	76
6.1	Template for questioning levels	119
6.2	Example using *Romeo and Juliet*	120
6.3	Example from health education	120
6.4	Example from business education	121

Acknowledgement

This book brings together a number of themes and interests: higher education policy, massification, social and educational diversity and disadvantage, and pedagogy.

I've worked in, and across, these areas for many years and in so doing have been extremely lucky to have worked and published with so many like-minded people. Most of the time, it has been extremely rewarding and often fun. So I'd like to pay my respects here to those who have helped me.

First and foremost I would like to thank Jim Donohue. I feel extremely fortunate to have come across his work and to have been taught by him, but also to have taught with him.

I'd also like to thank Evie Hiatt, Stacey Valdez and Debbie Shapiro from AVID for Higher Education. Thank you all for your generous sharing of your expertise and your constant good humour.

I would also like to thank Professor Joe Cuseo, Professor Emeritus of Psychology at Marymount College in California, from whom I learned about the psychological and emotional impact higher education has on students – particularly if their experiences are not good – and the powerful connection between this and university retention rates. As a Sociologist, these critical emotional perspectives were extremely useful in leading to a well-rounded understanding of the myriad influences which can either help or hinder a student's successful life at university – whatever their background.

The ethical responsibility academic staff have towards both their undergraduate and postgraduate students in terms of supporting them to success across diverse disciplines has been discussed with many colleagues and I thank them all: Professor Airini; Dr Paula Allman; Maxine Bradshaw; Associate Professor Barbara Brook; Dr Richard Chauvel; Dermot Clancy; Dr Lachlan Clohesy; Dr Tim Corcoran; Associate Professor Kerry Dickson; Professor Pat Drake; Andrew Ewing; Dr Gylo Hercelinskyj; Dr Robert Kazcan; Dr Sebastian Krook; Dr Jenny Lee; Associate Professor Mark McMahon; Associate Professor Sarah Paddle; Jennifer Piper; Jeannie Rea; Professor Kay Souter; Dr Glenn Spoors; Associate Professor Julie Stephens; Dr Kathy Tangalakis; Monika Taylor; Professor Kitty Te Riele; Deb Tyler; Dr John Wallis; Dr Julie White; and Dr Brian Zammit.

Thanks also go to Nathan Brumley for his efficient editing.

Finally, I'd like to thank David Lee whose lifelong interest in pedagogy and careful attention to the learning needs of young people have had such an impact. The long conversations about pedagogical work and the teaching moment, including the enjoyment which such work leads to, have sustained me.

Introduction

This book is designed for people interested in learning and teaching in the higher education sectors of Australia, New Zealand, the United Kingdom and the United States. All four countries differ greatly in the ways in which their higher education institutions are organised and the degree to which they are funded by governments, by philanthropy, and by the students themselves.

Despite these differences, they have all, over the last ten years, made a significant commitment to massifying higher education. That is to say, they are interested in having much greater numbers of their populations with undergraduate degrees. In so doing, they have provided access to university to many students who otherwise would not have gone.

This simple fact raises a number of challenges to university cultures, as it does to universities' teaching cultures.

Encouraging Diversity in Higher Education: Supporting Student Success is designed for those who work with, and in, diversity. It provides an overview of the changes to the international higher education sector, and the views of teaching staff, but also includes forty-five teaching strategies varying from the simple to the complex. These strategies are explicitly explained and described, and the rationale for their usage is discussed.

Chapter 1 (*The inclusive university?*) provides a detailed discussion of the national and international economic catalysts which combined to generate the changes made to the higher education sectors of Australia, New Zealand, the United Kingdom and the United States. It discusses the discourses about diversity in the field, and the ways in which universities at different ends of the league tables have approached the challenge to enrol greater numbers of diverse students.

Chapter 2 (*Teaching the taught*) discusses the work of teaching itself – what it means to staff, and the changes wrought on students. It includes data from a small research project with a purposeful yet diverse sample of twenty tertiary staff trained to use transparent pedagogies, who used them over a two-year period. They attest to their efficacy when used within universities at the bottom of the league tables for promoting both student engagement and student success.

Chapter 3 (*Building a dialogic classroom: names matter*) offers pragmatic strategies for developing and promoting a classroom culture which is dialogic, egalitarian, welcoming and which develops social capital. Many of these teaching strategies might appear puerile at first glance, but they are extremely effective as a means of engendering the sense of belonging and engagement to the teacher and other students which is essential to students' persistence.

Chapter 4 (*Improving academic literacies*) contains a number of effective, pragmatic teaching strategies which are designed to develop a precise skill set for students unsure about the protocols of scholarly thinking and writing. In the main, they take only ten to fifteen minutes to do, yet have the potential to significantly improve both the understanding and enactment of a range of academic literacies.

Chapter 5 (*Collaboration*) concentrates on the development of the social bonds developed early in the teaching session and explores ten teaching strategies from the simple to the more advanced. All are scaffolded exercises with the potential to be used across a wide range of disciplines to assist students to develop skills in working cooperatively with others.

Chapter 6 (*Thinking critically*) covers the most complex pedagogies insofar as they are designed to encourage students to be in a position to both think about and discuss their own cognition in terms of higher- and lower-order thinking. When able to do this, students gain a much greater understanding of the demands of higher education assessment methods – both formative and summative. With this, they are equipped to more purposefully plan their writing tasks and ultimately gain control over their grades.

It is hoped that these teaching strategies assist everyone working with contemporary students to enrich their teaching vocabulary whilst effectively dealing with the everyday classroom concerns which face everyone confronting a class of confused, yet hopeful, undergraduates.

Chapter 1

The inclusive university?

Introduction

Beginning with the ways in which higher education in the United Kingdom, Australia, New Zealand and the United States has been transformed in recent times, and the arguments used by government for that transformation, this chapter sets out the argument for the use of transparent pedagogies. It explores the economic causes of international massification in the West, which arose partly in response to the huge growth of higher education in non-OECD countries. It then examines the ways in which diversity and social inclusion, more generally, have been discussed in policy terms and in terms of the positioning of people deemed to be socially excluded.

The impact of massification on universities is then explored – in terms of both their relative positioning on league tables, and their various responses to widening the participation of first-in-family students. Which universities provide access? Are they evenly spread?

The chapter concludes with a discussion of neoliberalism's impact on the practices and protocols of universities, and more particularly, the ways in which universities can intercede to create the conditions whereby all students can experience a critical, transformative education which equips them with the skills to both 'read the world' but also act within it (Freire 2000; Tapp 2014).

Why massify?

Over the past ten years, there has been a growing international push, across almost every jurisdiction, for an increase in the proportion of people with a tertiary education in every population. The reasons for this are manifold. Its origins can perhaps be found in the global need for more educated citizens, most notably to meet the needs of changing economies, sometimes called 'knowledge' economies. These are economies which are increasingly reliant on technology, on the generation of knowledge and on the use of such knowledge for progress and growth. In this context, there is a growing need for employees with a range of both intellectual and practical skills found only through engagement in higher education (Bradley *et al.* 2008; Gorard *et al.* 2006; OECD 2012b; Teese 2000; Tight 2012). Considered from an individual's point of view, there seems little doubt that possessing an undergraduate degree substantially raises one's lifetime income and, conversely, not having a degree leaves one currently unable to join a growing number of professions – and this figure is increasing (Pew Research Center 2015).

But there is also data emerging from the OECD which highlights the ways in which the international market in higher education is changing – with higher education becoming increasingly established in non-OECD countries and the concomitant reduction of the numbers of international students travelling to study:

> In 2000, there were 51 million 25–34 year olds with higher education (tertiary) degrees in OECD countries, and 39 million in non-OECD G20 countries. Over the past decade, however, this gap has nearly closed, in large part because of the remarkable expansion of higher education in this latter group of countries. For example, in 2010 there were an estimated 66 million 25–34 year-olds with a tertiary degree in OECD countries, compared to 64 million in non-OECD countries. If this trend continues, the number of 25–34 year-olds from Argentina, Brazil, China, India, Indonesia, the Russian Federation, Saudi Arabia and South Africa with a higher education degree will be almost 40% higher than the number from all OECD countries by 2020.
>
> (OECD 2012b: 1)

This data points to two possibilities which have contributed to the drive for the massification of higher education in OECD countries: firstly, a compounding drop in the income drawn from international enrolments; secondly, a need to ensure that the OECD economies remain competitive – even dominant – in the face of rapidly expanding economies in what, previously, had been part of the developing world.

These are, very broadly, the reasons why higher education in the OECD has been massified, by which I mean that the tertiary education participation rate has purposefully been driven upwards by government policy and, as a result, universities are faced with teaching many more students than ever before (Allais 2014). The United Kingdom, for example, aimed to have educated to tertiary level 50 per cent of their population aged 18–30 by 2010 (Action on Access 2009), Australia aims to equip 40 per cent of people in the same age bracket with an undergraduate degree by 2025 (Bradley *et al.* 2008), the United States' goal is 60 per cent by 2020 (up from 39.3 per cent) (U.S. Dept. of Education 2015) and New Zealand's aspiration is to even further increase the numbers of its population having studied at university at undergraduate level by 2017 (currently almost 60 per cent) (New Zealand Ministry of Education 2014). A few industrialised nations have even raised their participation rate to above 80 per cent of their population (Collins 2013). Arguably then, higher education has shifted from being an endeavour of the elite where less than 10 per cent of the population gained tertiary qualifications to an endeavour of the masses, where many more do.

This growth began in the post-war period, for the most part, and accelerated through the 1970s. It became clear that economies were changing and needed a more educated and technically skilled workforce than before. But also, student populations needed to be expanded. This was in order not only to meet the new workforce needs, but also in response to pressure from feminism, the left and the black rights movement who saw university education as an elite, white, masculine pursuit and sought to have it democratised. This was broadly achieved both through increasing the numbers of women and people of colour who attended universities, but also through the broadening of curricula in order that the histories of subjugated people, for example, were studied alongside those of the elite (see Kelly & Slaughter 1991; Rogers 2012).

Tight (2012) points out that in the United Kingdom, for example, specific student cohorts were targeted for higher education participation at particular points in time, including working class people, women, the mature-aged and ethnic minorities (p. 212).[1] The building of these categories sits in stark contrast to the prototypical traditional student of the time for whom universities were originally designed, and who enjoyed a smooth entry into university, and then into professional careers: young, male, well-off and white.

After the war, in particular, growth in the tertiary sector addressed both the demographic shifts stemming from the fact that there were simply more young people following the post-war baby boom, and the need to differentiate and advance the newly emerging middle classes (Armstrong *et al.* 2011). Rather more ambitiously, higher education was – and still is – seen as a strategic means to generate firmer social cohesion through developing a more well-informed public with a shared set of democratic values. This, it was thought, would lead to stronger civic engagement (Armstrong & Cairnduff 2012).

Forty years later, such targeting continues, with New Zealand seeking to rapidly increase the numbers of Māori and Pasifika graduates (Cram *et al.* 2014), Australia steering people from low socioeconomic backgrounds into universities (Bradley 2008) and the United Kingdom spending £2 billion attempting to widen the participation of Black, ethnic minority and working-class students (Gorard 2008). In the United States, depending on state, they are attempting to close the currently large gap between the graduation rates of Black and Latino[2] students and all others (Rooks 2006). Of course, it can also be argued that through universities' bid to grow student numbers, they have behaved like any other corporation that seeks to expand its consumer base in order to improve its market share, and thus compete more effectively with its rivals. This, in turn, can lead to improvements in its position on a range of league tables, which is very appealing to any university (Turner 2005; Usher & Savino 2007).

Discursive positioning about diversity

Alongside these broadly economic causes and effects of massification, governments have sought to explain and promote their policy approaches to the higher education sector largely through the use of discourses which foster a sense of altruism and social responsibility (Archer 2007; Armstrong *et al.* 2011; Hughes 2015; Mavelli 2014; Palmer *et al.* 2011; Sheeran *et al.* 2007).

Arguments about increased educational levels leading to increased civil responsibility and democracy have come from various sources but they all share the common notion that healthy economies are those which have invested in the growth of their human capital (Abbott-Chapman 2011; Action on Access 2009; Gorard *et al.* 2006; OECD 2012a). It is argued that economic development is fuelled as much by the improved civic participation resulting from a more educated populace, as it is by stronger, more innovative, more intelligent knowledge economies. Likewise, others have argued that on an individual level, simply having graduated from a university leads to a pronounced improvement in any individual's sense of life satisfaction in general, their sense of meaning in life, usefulness and security, their sense of wellbeing, their health status – in addition to much higher lifetime earnings (Abbott-Chapman 2011; Marginson 1997).

But within this discursive field of diversity or social inclusion, how are the various non-university-going groups positioned? How are they viewed by government? By policy? By universities themselves?

One answer to this series of questions is that they are perceived as inherently problematic, almost incapable of making rational decisions, and ignorant of the decisions which would be of most benefit to them (hence their non-attendance at school/university). Of course, as any sociologist will tell you, it is much more complex than this – students and potential students from non-university-going backgrounds also make sets of decisions about their education, and sometimes they perceive tertiary education as an almost hostile environment, or at the very least, one which does not place value on their lives or experiences (Abbott-Chapman 2011; Archer & Hutchings 2000; Ballantyne *et al.* 2009; Bowden & Doughney 2010; Christie *et al.* 2008; Collier & Morgan 2008; Dennis *et al.* 2005; Devlin 2011; Hughes 2015; Lehmann 2009; McCarron & Inkelas 2006; Morrison 2010; Murphy 2009; Pearce *et al.* 2008; Read *et al.* 2003; Schuetze & Slowey 2003; Watt *et al.* 2011). Within this context, 'aspiration' has become key and is used to explain the traditionally relatively low levels of higher education participation by particular demographic cohorts.

As Sellar *et al.* (2011) explain:

> However, 'raising aspiration' is a deeply problematic trope around which to establish social justice projects. There are at least three aspects of concern here. First, dominant conceptions of aspiration imply potentially offensive and normative assumptions about the value and legitimacy of particular educational pathways, forms of employment and life projects. That is, those who don't aspire to higher education are assumed to have lower aspirations. Second, it underestimates the potential for stratification associated with expanding education systems, which can result in less advantaged students being diverted into lower status institutions. ... Third, it is by no means clear that

underrepresentation in HE is caused by low aspiration, as opposed to holding aspirations for different ends or not having the capacity to realise one's aspirations.

(p. 38)

Conversely, in the discursive field of government policy, those without a tertiary education are conceived of as being – or becoming – a cost to the taxpayer through not equipping themselves for productive professional careers or paying the accompanying taxes, not participating in civil society (in a broad sense) and in turn, not preparing their children to as fully engage in education and work as they should. North and Ferrier (2009), for example, using data from the Australian Bureau of Statistics, argue that 'socially excluded' people have tangible results in their lives which include:

- Being dependent on government support as their main income source
- Having multiple children
- Having a lack of access to a car and
- Being unable to access the Internet at home (p. 45)

The financial imperative to increase the numbers of student enrolments becomes even more acute when one considers that students in Australia, the United Kingdom and New Zealand are increasingly bearing more of the financial burden of their university education as students in the United States do. They become a source of revenue for governments increasingly relieved of the financial burden of universities – rather in the same way that international education has become a very significant source of income for many OECD countries, in particular (OECD 2014).

The diversity conundrum

The governments of Australia, New Zealand, the United Kingdom and the United States have shaped their higher education policies around a number of intersected strategies:

- reduced funding of universities offset by the increased financial responsibility of students for their education
- targeting specific demographic cohorts from non-university-going backgrounds for university entrance
- reduction of spending on government benefits by increasing the earning power of the socially disadvantaged and
- concomitant increases in revenue from taxation.

But what does this massification mean for the universities themselves?

Firstly, whilst these economic strategies are in place, discourses of diversity become an almost moral imperative and have been used, in part, as an explanation for the policies of widening participation and social inclusion. Louise Archer (2007), for example, has argued that the use of 'diversity' (now inseparably linked to the endeavour of widening participation in higher education for the reasons already outlined) acts as a compelling discourse insofar as its contestation becomes almost impossible (p. 648). In this context, the demographic groupings which are the least likely to be university-going are the most likely to be constituted as of in need of social inclusion via higher education. Here, they are perceived of as the worthy Other in need of a catalyst for transition into a tax-paying profession and all the benefits which arise from that (Allais 2014).

One of the important consequences of this discursive positioning is the way in which it neatly individualises structural, social inequalities. So, for example, the actual sources of educational drop-out (the habitus and aspirations of the secondary schools which 'diverse' students attend, for example, or the financial reasons why they leave education and gain premature employment) are obscured (Bourdieu & Wacquant 1992; Gale & Mills 2013; Gorard et al. 2006; Hughes 2015; Lehmann 2009; Mavelli 2014; Pearce et al. 2008; Wilkins & Burke 2013). This in turn leads to the sense that a non-tertiary-educated individual from a non-university-going background is in fact a logical and individualistic consumer, but one whose consumption lies in the future rather than in the past. They are a neoliberal subject – with many apparent choices about their educational and working lives (Archer 2007). A logical conclusion to such reasoning, of course, is that if the subject chooses not to avail themselves of the many educational opportunities presented to them, then they are simply at fault.

The university Olympics

Massification, whilst an international development, impacts on universities in different ways – and to varying extents. For the most part, students from non-university-going backgrounds are given access to non-elite universities which have made their access requirements more permeable through dropping their entry requirements (Forsyth & Furlong 2003), through building stronger partnerships with the school sector and providing students with advanced credit of various kinds (Hughes & Brown 2014) or through offering a wider range of entry points and methods (Palmer et al. 2011). Elite universities might similarly offer scholarships, or special entrance or study programs but their student bodies tend to remain relatively stable (McManus et al. 2012). This should perhaps not come as a surprise given that such universities have built their reputations on their ability to recruit the 'best', to remain inaccessible to the majority of students and to neglect the rest (see Norrie 2012).

Perhaps partly as a result of post-war massification, and partly due to the increased use of, and interest in, relative league tables (Turner 2005; Usher & Savino 2007), there has been an increased stratification of universities in the United Kingdom, Australia, the United States and New Zealand.

Archer (2007) builds a convincing picture of the sector, drawing on universities in the United Kingdom but using a metaphor equally applicable elsewhere. She argues that there are three tiers in the sector – gold, silver and bronze – each distinguished by a common set of characteristics and aspirations.

Those ranked 'gold' are primarily orientated towards a global market, and towards attracting both elite staff and elite students from a strong reputational base and position within world rankings such as the Times Higher Education World Rankings, the Shanghai Jiao Tong Ranking and the QS World University Rankings.[3] They are international in focus and, perhaps unsurprisingly, strongly motivated to move upwards in the league tables through shaping their activities towards excellence in the ranking criteria (indeed, the QS World University Rankings uses international orientation as one of its rating methods).

The second-ranked 'silver' universities are more nationally focussed, but with some international orientation, and are therefore dedicated to attaining robust national reputations for overall excellence measured by research output and quality, primarily. They promote themselves as solid performers and, on occasion, use their ranking for learning and teaching quality as a measure of their success. In turn, they aim to become 'gold' through attention to the ranking criteria and, in particular, through the recruitment of international staff with strong reputations whose presence will, in turn, boost the status of the university. Largely, in the case of 'silver' universities, they are interested in competing against national rather than international rivals.

Finally, 'bronze' universities are the remainder. In the United Kingdom they are termed 'post-1992' since their origins were commonly Polytechnics or the Colleges of Higher Education which were renamed after the Further and Higher Education Act of 1992. Similarly, Australia's Colleges of Advanced Education were morphed (and sometimes amalgamated) into universities in 1989 and are commonly called 'Post-Dawkins' after the Minister for Education who restructured the tertiary sector. New Zealand historically has had the most egalitarian higher education sector, although some of its eight universities have similarly arisen from other institutions and been granted university status. Nevertheless, a ranking exists based on the conventional ranking criteria (see Ranking Web 2015). The United States has a more complex tertiary system, but one which is inexorably bound up with both world rankings[4] and 'Ivy League' traditions. For the purposes here, I suggest that 'bronze' universities in the United States are public institutions, rather than private, and ones whose population has relatively higher numbers of Black and Latino students.

Bronze universities commonly have a mission concentrated on serving their local communities from where they frequently draw their students, often because their reputation is not strong enough to attract students from other parts of the country, unlike their 'gold' peers. They usually serve 'diverse' communities in educationally disadvantaged regions. Naturally, their ambitions trend upwards too, to national recognition for excellence in teaching and research (Archer 2007: 640).

Given this, it is perhaps unsurprising that it is the 'bronze' universities who are enrolling large numbers of students from non-university-going backgrounds. In Australia, for example, the national goal of having 20 per cent of all undergraduate students from low socioeconomic status (SES) backgrounds, which was put in place in 2008, is shouldered most unevenly across the different tiers in the sector. 'Gold' universities have between four and fourteen per cent participation rates of low-SES students, 'silver' between eleven and seventeen per cent, and 'bronze' universities between fifteen and fifty-three per cent (McManus et al. 2012).[5]

How might universities best meet the needs of students?

Let's focus now on the universities that are dedicated to teaching, and teaching well, large numbers of first-in-family students who are entering tertiary education for the first time, often without the full range of social, cultural and educational capital which make university a comfortable and easy place to be – skills which more traditional students commonly enjoy as a matter of course.

But firstly, let's be clear about the sorts of literacies and levels of social and cultural capital universities commonly assume their incoming students have. Lawrence (2005) offers a concise list of these, arguing that:

> Each subject has its specific prerequisites and/or assumed entry knowledge; subject matter (content or process orientated, text-bound, oral or computer-mediated); language; texts (study packages, lecture notes, PowerPoint notes, web CT documents, CD Rom); cultural practices (ways of dressing and showing respect – Professor, first names); attendance [mode] (lectures, tutorials, practical sessions, clinical sessions, external/internal/online); behaviours (rule-governed/flexible, compulsory/optional attendance, consultation times, electronic discussion groups); class participation (passive, interactive, experiential); rules (about extensions, participation, resubmissions, appeals); theoretical assumptions (scientific/sociological); research methodologies (positivist/interpretive/critical, quantitative/qualitative); ways of thinking (recall, reflective, analytical or critical, surface or deep); referencing systems (APA, Harvard, MLA); ways of writing (essays/reports/journals/orals); structure (particularly in relation to assessment); tone and style (word choice, active/passive voice, third/second/first person, sentence structure, paragraph structure); formatting (left/right justified, font, type, spacing, margins); assessment (exams, assignments, orals, formative/summative, individual/group).
>
> (p. 247)

All students will have partial understanding of these many protocols, but the extent and depth of their understanding will heavily depend on whether they come from university-going backgrounds where they have imbibed educational capital from an early age and approach university with confidence, or whether these protocols are quite new to them (Devlin et al. 2012). Irrespective of their levels and breadth of understanding, for the most part, universities have traditionally anticipated that new undergraduates will come to navigate these protocols fairly quickly, and without direct communication about the expected conventions (although referencing systems are commonly an exception!).

How are the different university tiers responding to the needs of incoming students for whom tertiary protocols are, at the very least, obscure or confusing? There seems little doubt that each tier is responding to the comparative requirements of each student intake. For many, there is a concentration of student-facing remedial study skills support systems put in place by those working to quickly equip students with the literacies listed by Lawrence. These generically take the form of 'uni-ready' summer schools, study skills seminars as part of orientation, peer mentoring systems and so forth (Peach 2005). Similarly, many universities encourage (or commit) their staff to enrol in a higher education teaching certificate or diploma (Gibbs 2013).

Internationally, the tertiary sector is undergoing dramatic change through massification, and for some universities the changes are profound both in terms of the numbers of students enrolling, and in terms of their preparedness for university (Abbott-Chapman 2011; Abramson & Jones 2003; Ballantyne et al. 2009; Bowser & Danaher 2007; Christie et al. 2008; Collier & Morgan 2008; Murphy 2009). Others develop discourses of social inclusion and greater access for 'diverse' students whilst not shifting their pedagogies in order to assist students to transition into university cultures. So although participation is being widened internationally, across tertiary sectors en masse, participation is far wider in some institutions than others. One consequence of this unevenness is the maintenance of the university Olympic system where lower-ranked universities remain bronze because their efforts are commonly focussed on serving the needs of diverse students with good teaching, rather than on establishing reputations for research excellence which would more effectively raise their international and domestic rankings in the league tables.

Silver and bronze universities, however, are much more likely to engage in professionally developing their teaching staff in order to better address the lack of fit which students from low-SES backgrounds report, in particular, and which is borne out by their much higher levels of attrition (see Devlin et al. 2012). Critically, these universities are endeavouring to better provide for their students and strategically move away from traditional learning and teaching practices which have obscured the hidden curriculum (Abramson & Jones 2003; Allen et al. 2008; Ballantyne et al. 2009; Bowser & Danaher 2007; Clegg et al. 2006; Kift et al. 2010; Leach 2011; Murphy 2009; Peach 2005; Schuetze & Slowey 2003).

Neoliberalism and higher education

Higher education not only has felt the impact of international massification, it is also experiencing a more profound assault on the core values which dominated the sector for centuries. In short, these were values which perceived higher education as a good in itself, and universities as key institutions which not only produced and disseminated new knowledge but were pivotal to healthy, democratic societies where citizens were entitled to high levels of civic participation. Latterly they have also been extolled as institutions which create high levels of social mobility. Indeed, as discussed earlier, government policies have explicitly been organised to bring such social mobility about.

Higher education is in the midst of dramatic change as it becomes progressively compelled by neoliberal discourses and practices which mean higher education is increasingly drawn into the purview of the free market and subject to its principles (Allais 2014; Williams 2012). Neoliberalising processes begin from the belief and assertion that market principles should manage social relationships and proceed by compelling or convincing institutions and their staff to organise themselves in this way (Amsler 2014; Harvey 2007). As Jenkins (2014) explains:

> Neoliberalism – a term now used only by critics – evokes the absorption of the erstwhile social state into a corporate culture. The purported minimisation of the scope of political power corresponds to the ascendency of economic man [sic], characterised by entrepreneurial spirit, individualism, flexibility and adaptability. Appeals to economic rationality and practical constraints, and the use of words like 'performance', 'efficiency', 'mobility', 'competitiveness' and 'evaluation', cast mockery at institutions modelled on solidarity, social security, justice or the substantive values of democracy. What lacks market value also lacks the right to exist. The university, to survive, must engage in benchmarking, marketing; seek public-private partnerships; generate profits; incentivise its employees; and offer up its technocratic expert knowledge, as evidence of its co-operative participation in presumptively necessary processes of change.
>
> (p. 49)

It is within this context that it has been argued that the neoliberal shift underway is fundamentally reshaping higher education and changing it from an endeavour designed to increase private and public good in the broadest sense, to one like any other company in the marketplace but one designed to increase the marketability and employability of those who have bought its services (Amsler 2014; Archer 2007; Mavelli 2014; Sutton 2014).

This is the context in which massification is taking place. As discussed earlier, the United Kingdom, New Zealand and Australia have all engaged in large-scale attempts to give access to higher education to people from non-university-going backgrounds who ordinarily would neither have aspired to go nor had the entrance qualifications. Universities have both loosened their entrance requirements and partnered with schools in traditionally educationally disadvantaged areas to encourage their students to go to university, and hopefully to graduate – with demographic groupings and national targets established (Action on Access 2009; Bowden & Doughney 2010; Bradley *et al.* 2008; Forsyth & Furlong 2003; Hughes & Brown 2014; Morrison 2010; Sellar *et al.* 2011).

These endeavours are often claimed to be critical to social mobility, and to increasing social inclusion through equipping students for the employment demands of neoliberal knowledge economies (Archer 2007; Bradley *et al.* 2008; Cram *et al.* 2014; Hughes 2015; North & Ferrier 2009; OECD 2012a; Pew Research Center 2015). But they also further neoliberal economies not only through the private investment in human capital, but also through the dissemination of neoliberal reasoning and managerialism (Amsler 2014; Bowl 2010; Brown 2009; Mavelli 2014; Wilkins & Burke 2013; Williams 2012).

Indeed, Clegg (2008) offers the bleak argument that neoliberalism effectively requisitioned the United Kingdom's innovative Widening Participation project which aimed to increase access to higher education for many more students. She argues that this worthwhile ambition was replaced by individualism, which promoted consumerism. In other words, the material accumulation which would result from the gaining of a degree became the rationale for widening participation, rather than the social benefits resulting from having a more educated populace. There have been varied results from these initiatives. The demographic characteristics of those being admitted to higher education have not been as diverse as hoped, and universities have often been unable to keep them to completion (Forsyth & Furlong 2003; Gorard 2008; Hughes 2015; Tight 2012).

Pedagogical work

Universities are in a state of seemingly unending turmoil, often operating both an *ancien regime* and a modern, neoliberal corporation with an eye perpetually on competitors. In the following chapter, there is an exploration of the impact of these conflicting impulses on academics themselves. But, for now, let's turn to the most overlooked yet most important part of higher education – the classroom.

Bourdieu and Passeron first used the term 'pedagogical work' in the 1970s, arguing that pedagogy is both a communication and a power system and as such plays a key role in the ways in which individual students are changed through their engagement with universities – not simply through what they learn, but the ways in which they learn it (Bourdieu & Passeron 1977). Even within the contemporary neoliberal university, with its compelling arguments about research excellence and career progression, pedagogical work itself can be organised to be purposefully transformative, sometimes for staff as well as students. For many educators interested in critical education, their standpoint is most seriously challenged by neoliberal discourse and the practices which result from it (Archer 2008). Foremost amongst these is the awkward truth that teaching in higher education is the least rewarded, and least acknowledged, part of any academic's workload. Furthermore, being teaching-focussed tends to be detrimental to early or mid-career academics amidst the increasing pressure for research productivity. Time spent preparing excellent classes or, equally importantly, providing students with the contact and support which better secure their success is time not spent on research or administrative matters (Richardson & Radloff 2014). In short, good teaching is largely perceived as being of secondary importance in higher education, despite many universities' proclamations to the contrary, and the key cause of this is each university's drive to climb the league tables, which is achieved through increasing both the volume and quality of research output (Turner 2005; Usher & Savino 2007).

Using a neoliberal logic, universities have commonly responded to the need for research output by effectively splitting the traditional academic position where one both teaches and researches into two – with greater specialisation. There are more research-only positions (frequently short-term, grant-dependent contracts), more staff appointed to teaching-only positions (commonly known as 'teaching scholars') and more casual teaching staff on short-term contracts. In many university departments, the latter group undertake most of the larger teaching load which widening participation has produced and yet they occupy a marginal space within the academy – not really part of it given their temporary work contracts, yet not separate (Brown *et al.* 2013; May *et al.* 2013; Richardson & Radloff 2014). These staff also find their employment entirely dependent on the vagaries of student demand for courses and it can vary substantially throughout the academic year. Archer (2008) argues that one of the key features of the neoliberal subject is its elasticity, its flexibility – a subject who can, and must, adapt to reduced or expanded employment opportunities as the market demands. Casual university teaching staff are exemplars of this as market principles have come to reorder and reform what was arguably the core of higher education – the relationship between students and staff (Amsler 2014). Yet relationships between staff and students persist, of course, and pedagogical work goes on every day in hundreds of thousands of university classrooms all over the world. Perhaps what really matters is how this pedagogical work is done, and despite the gloomy picture of the practices of neoliberal universities painted earlier, there is still (to date) a comparative freedom to what happens in classrooms, despite the student evaluations which follow. Clegg (2008), for example, argues that:

> Despite all the pressure of performativity, individuals have created spaces for the exercise of principled personal autonomy and agency. This should perhaps not surprise us if we start from the theoretical assumptions about the importance of theorising self and agency.
>
> (p. 343)

If one treats the classroom as a 'created space', and careful thought is given to the pedagogical work which occurs there, then there is an argument to be made that despite, or because of, the constraints placed around the modern university, the classroom can be used as a transformative space.

Of course, it would be impossible to find anybody who works in higher education who disputed the base argument that high participation rates in higher education generate both individual and social transformation (Action on Access 2009; Bradley *et al.* 2008; Gale & Parker 2013; Sutton 2014). Quite how this transformation is produced is more problematic, but Michel Foucault's discussion of the distinction between *savoir* and *connaissance* can assist in conceptualising two discrete ways of perceiving pedagogical work – in short, these terms refer to process and product (Foucault 1991; Foucault 2005; Mavelli 2014). *Savoir,* according to Foucault, is a slow process of transformation, where the manner of coming to conceptualise something, the unhurried process of understanding, inexorably leads to a scholar whose subjectivity has been inexorably and inevitably altered. Sutton (2014) convincingly contests that 'It is the ontological state of being unfinished that makes us educable' (p. 41). *Connaissance,* on the other hand, refers to knowledge which is detached from the knower – it is a package for sale. Like Freire's 'banked' knowledge (Freire 2000) it is in effect seen as a commodity to be purchased from a university. In neoliberal economies, this is the keystone of the economic exchange between university and student. In this context, knowledge is perceived of as tangential to the learner whose subjectivity remains unchanged (Mavelli 2014). For the purposes of this book, it is *savoir,* the process of understanding, the coming to knowledge and the permeability of knowledge, which is of interest. How can educators generate transformative classrooms under neoliberalism?

Thomson (as quoted in Sheeran *et al.* 2007) offers one answer to this question:

> The challenge presented by widening participation in higher education ... is not in our view about 'helping' the socially excluded; or squeezing more non-traditional students into increasingly overcrowded lecture theatres ... rather it is about developing a sustained critique of current rhetoric, developing a distinctive social theory of knowledge derived from a politically committed analysis and theory of power which leads to a form of pedagogy that is concerned to democratize knowledge and learning, in ways that redefine the very parameters of what counts as higher education.
>
> (p. 255)

This book explores the use of transparent pedagogies as one way to bring to fruition the democratisation of knowledge and learning which Thomson believes is possible – within a neoliberal framework. Even with the fiscal, discursive and structural alterations which have beset universities in the United Kingdom, the United States, New Zealand and Australia, it is possible to create classrooms where higher education students do indeed learn to engage critically with their world.

Whilst there is no shortage of literature written about pedagogy in higher education in the broadest sense (Amsler 2014; Canaan 2005; Gale & Mills 2013; Haggis 2006; Ramsden 2003; Roberts 2011) there is nevertheless a gap in the literature where classroom pragmatics are both theorised and discussed. More particularly, there is also little known about the perceptions of educators working under neoliberalism whilst also attached to the notion that higher education can – and should – indeed be transformative.

In the next chapter, there is a focus on precisely these issues that builds the case for the use of transparent pedagogies. It also explores the perceptions of a range of academics who have used them.

Notes

1 These are not discrete categories of course.
2 Latino refers to people from Spanish-speaking cultures who are American.
3 The QS World University Rankings are compiled through academic peer review, faculty–student ratio, citations per faculty, recruiter review and international orientation.
4 Interestingly, the 'College Admissions Rate' ranking rates universities on the ratio between application and admission. See http://www.washingtonpost.com/local/education/college-admission-rates-for-class-of-2018-an-imperfect-but-closely-watched-metric/2014/04/03/820ff578-b6af-11e3-8cc3-d4bf596577eb_story.html
5 This was determined by my 'banding' the overall ranking of the thirty-nine universities into three according to their longevity and their national ranking.

Bibliography

Abbott-Chapman, J. (2011) 'Making the most of the mosaic: Facilitating post-school transitions to higher education of disadvantaged students', *Australian Educational Researcher* 38(1): 57–71.

Abramson, M. & P. Jones (2003) 'Tinto's model of retention revisited: A case study from a "new" British university', in L. Thomas, M. Cooper & J. Quinn (eds) *Improving completion rates among disadvantaged students*, Stoke on Trent, UK: Trentham Books, pp. 133–148.

Action on Access (2009) *Mainstreaming and Sustaining Widening Participation in Institutions*. Final Report to the Higher Education Funding Council for England.

Allais, S. (2014) 'A critical perspective on large class teaching: The political economy of massification and the sociology of knowledge', *Higher Education* 67(6): 721–734.

Allen, J., S.B. Robbins, A. Casillas & I. Oh (2008) 'Third-year college retention and transfer: Effects of academic performance, motivation, and social connectedness', *Research in Higher Education* 49(7): 647–664.

Amsler, S. (2014) '"By ones and twos and tens": Pedagogies of possibility for democratising higher education', *Pedagogy, Culture and Society* 22(2): 275–294.

Archer, L. (2007) 'Diversity, equality and higher education: A critical reflection on the ab/uses of equity discourse within widening participation', *Teaching in Higher Education* 12(5–6): 635–653.

Archer, L. (2008) 'The new neoliberal subjects? Younger academics' constructions of professional identity', *Journal of Educational Policy* 23(3): 265–285.

Archer, L. & M. Hutchings (2000) '"Bettering yourself"? Discourses of risk, cost and benefit in ethnically diverse, young working-class non-participants' constructions of higher education', *British Journal of Sociology of Education*, 21(4): 555–574.

Armstrong, D., A.C. Armstrong & I. Spandagou (2011) 'Inclusion: By choice or by chance?', *International Journal of Inclusive Education* 15(1): 29–39.

Armstrong, D. & A. Cairnduff (2012) 'Inclusion in higher education: Issues in university–school partnership', *International Journal of Inclusive Education* 16(9): 917–928.

Ballantyne, J., T. Madden & N. Todd (2009) 'Gauging the attitudes of non-traditional students at a new campus: An Australian case study', *Journal of Higher Education Policy and Management* 31(4): 301–313.

Bourdieu, P. & J.C. Passeron (1977) *Reproduction in Education, Society and Culture*, London: Sage.

Bourdieu, P. & L. Wacquant (1992) *An Invitation to Reflexive Sociology*, Cambridge: Polity Press.

Bowden, M.P. & J. Doughney (2010) 'Socioeconomic status, cultural diversity and the aspirations of secondary students in the western suburbs of Melbourne, Australia', *Higher Education* 51(9): 115–129.

Bowl, M. (2010) 'University continuing education in a neoliberal landscape: Developments in England and Aotearoa New Zealand', *International Journal of Lifelong Education* 29(6): 723–738.

Bowser, D. & P.A. Danaher (2007) 'Indigenous, pre-undergraduate and international students at Central Queensland University, Australia: Three cases of the dynamic tension between diversity and commonality', *Teaching in Higher Education* 12(5&6): 669–681.

Bradley, D., P. Noonan, H. Nugent & B. Scales (2008) *Review of Australian Higher Education, Final Report*, Canberra: Commonwealth Government.

Brown, N.R., J.A. Kelder, B. Freeman & A.R. Carr (2013) 'A message from the chalk face: What casual teaching staff tell us they want to know, access and experience', *Journal of University Teaching and Learning Practice* 10(3). http://ro.uow.edu.au/cgi/viewcontent.cgi?article=1380&context=jutlp. Accessed 17 March 2016.

Brown, W. (2009) 'Neoliberalism and the end of liberal democracy', in *Edgework: Critical Essays on Knowledge and Politics*, Princeton, NJ: Princeton University Press, pp. 37–59.

Canaan, J. (2005) 'Developing a pedagogy of critical hope', *Learning and Teaching in the Social Sciences* 2(3): 159–174.

Christie, H., L. Tett, V.E. Cree, J. Hounsell & V. McCune (2008) '"A real rollercoaster of confidence and emotions": Learning to be a university student', *Studies in Higher Education* 33(5): 567–581.

Clegg, S. (2008) 'Academic identities under threat?', *British Educational Research Journal* 34(3): 329–345.

Clegg, S., S. Bradley & K. Smith (2006) '"I've had to swallow my pride": Help seeking and self-esteem', *Higher Education Research and Development* 25(2): 101–113.

Collier, P.J. & D.L. Morgan (2008) '"Is that paper really due today?" Differences in first-generation and traditional college students' understandings of faculty expectations', *Higher Education* 55(4): 425–446.

Collins, R. (2013) 'The end of middle-class work: No more escapes', in I. Wallerstein, R. Collins, M. Mann, G. Derluguian, & C. Calhoun (eds.), *Does Capitalism Have a Future?* Oxford: Oxford University Press, pp. 37–70.

Cram, F., H. Phillips, P. Sauni & C. Tuagalu (eds) (2014) *Māori and Pasifika Higher Education Horizons* (Diversity in Higher Education, Volume 15), Bingley, UK: Emerald Group Publishing Limited.

Dennis, J.M., J.S. Phinney & L.I. Chuateco (2005) 'The role of motivation, parental support, and peer support in the academic success of ethnic minority first-generation college students', *Journal of College Student Development* 46(3): 223–236.

Devlin, M. (2011) 'Bridging socio-cultural incongruity: Conceptualising the success of students from low socio-economic status backgrounds in Australian higher education', *Studies in Higher Education* 38(6): 939–949.

Devlin, M., S. Kift, K. Nelson, L. Smith & J. McKay (2012) *Effective Teaching and Support of Students from Low Socioeconomic Backgrounds. Resources for Australian Higher Education.* http://www.lowses.edu.au/. Accessed 13 April 2015.

Forsyth, A. & A. Furlong (2003) 'Access to higher education and disadvantaged young people', *British Educational Research Journal* 29(2): 205–225.

Foucault, M. (1991) *Remarks on Marx*, translated by J.R. Goldstein & J. Cascaito. New York: Semiotext(e).

Foucault, M. (2005) *The Hermeneutics of the Subject: Lectures at the Collège de France 1981–1982*, New York: Picador.
Freire, P. (2000) *Pedagogy of the Oppressed*, New York: Continuum.
Gale, T. & C. Mills (2013) 'Creating spaces in higher education for marginalised Australians: Principles for socially inclusive pedagogies', *Enhancing Learning in the Social Sciences* 5(2): 7–19.
Gale, T. & S. Parker (2013) *Widening Participation in Australian Higher Education*. A report submitted to the Higher Education Funding Council for England (HEFCE) and the Office for Fair Access (OFFA), England, Leicester, UK: CFE (Research and Consulting) Ltd., Ormskirk, UK: Edge Hill University.
Gibbs, G. (2013) 'Reflections on the changing nature of educational development', *International Journal for Academic Development* 18(1): 4–14.
Gorard, S. (2008) 'Who is missing from higher education?', *Cambridge Journal of Education* 38(3): 421–437.
Gorard, S., E. Smith, H. May, L. Thomas, N. Adnett & K. Slack (2006) *Review of Widening Participation Research: Addressing the Barriers to Participation in Higher Education*, Bristol: Higher Education Funding Council for England.
Haggis, T. (2006) 'Pedagogies for diversity: Retaining critical challenge amidst fears of "dumbing down"', *Studies in Higher Education* 31(5): 521–535.
Harvey, D. (2007) *A Brief History of Neoliberalism*, Oxford: Oxford University Press.
Hughes, K. (2015) 'The social inclusion meme in higher education: Are universities doing enough?', *International Journal of Inclusive Education* 19(3): 303–313.
Hughes, K. & C. Brown (2014) 'Strengthening the intersections between secondary and tertiary education in Australia: Building cultural capital', *Journal of University Teaching & Learning Practice*, 11(2): http://ro.uow.edu.au/jutlp/vol11/iss2/6.
Jenkins, F. (2014) 'Gendered hierarchies of knowledge and the prestige factor: How philosophy survives market rationality', in M. Thornton (ed), *Through a Glass Darkly: The Social Sciences Look at the Neoliberal University*, Canberra: ANU Press, pp. 49–62.
Kelly, G.P. & S. Slaughter (1991) *Women's Higher Education in Comparative Perspective*, Dordrecht: Kluwer.
Kift, S.M., K.J. Nelson & J.A. Clarke (2010) 'Transition pedagogy: A third generation approach to FYE: A case study of policy and practice for the higher education sector', *The International Journal of the First Year in Higher Education* 1(1): 1–20.
Lawrence, J. (2005) 'Addressing diversity in higher education: Two models for facilitating student engagement and mastery', in A. Brew & C. Asmar (eds), *Higher Education in a Changing World. Research and Development in Higher Education, 28. Proceedings of the 2005 HERDSA Annual Conference*, Sydney: University of Sydney, pp. 243–252.
Leach, L. (2011) '"I treat all students as equal": Further and higher education teachers' responses to diversity', *Journal of Further and Higher Education* 35(2): 247–263.
Lehmann, W. (2009) 'Becoming middle class: How working class university students draw and transgress moral class boundaries', *Sociology* 43(4): 631–647.
Marginson, S. (1997) *Educating Australia: Government, Economy and Citizenship since 1960*, Melbourne: Cambridge University Press.
Mavelli, L. (2014) 'Widening participation, the instrumentalization of knowledge and the reproduction of inequality', *Teaching in Higher Education* 19(8): 860–869.
May, R., G. Strahan & D. Peetz (2013) 'Workforce development and renewal in Australian universities and the management of casual academic staff', *Journal of University Teaching and Learning Practice* 10(3): http://ro.uow.edu.au/jutlp/vol10/iss3/3.

McCarron, G.P. & K.K. Inkelas (2006) 'The gap between educational aspirations and attainment for first-generation college students and the role of parental involvement', *Journal of College Student Development*, 47(5): 534–549.

McManus, M.E., C. Shannon, A. Lee, M. Fairman & C. Hourigan (2012) *Beyond Bias and Stereotypes in Student Recruitment: Providing Pathways for All Australians*, Paper presented at the *Social Inclusion in Higher Education* conference, Melbourne, 27–28 September.

Morrison, A. (2010) '"I want an education": Two cases of working class ambition and ambivalence in further and higher education', *Research in Post-Compulsory Education* 15(1): 175–185.

Murphy, B. (2009) 'Great expectations? Progression and achievement of less traditional entrants to higher education', *Widening Participation and Lifelong Learning* 11(2): 4–14.

New Zealand Ministry of Education (2014) *Tertiary Education Strategy*, http://www.education.govt.nz/ministry-of-education/overall-strategies-and-policies/tertiary-education-strategy. Accessed 13 April 2015.

Norrie, J. (2012) University standards at risk from low performing school leavers, https://theconversation.edu.au/university-standards-at-risk-from-low-performing-school-leavers-5697. Accessed 20 March 2015.

North, S. & F. Ferrier (2009) *Review of Vocational Education and Training Research in Australia 2008–2009*, Report prepared for Department of Education, Employment and Workplace Relations. Monash University, Melbourne: Centre for the Economics of Education and Training.

OECD (2012a) *Equity and Quality in Education. Supporting Disadvantaged Students and Schools*, http://dx.doi.org/10.1787/9789264130852-en. Accessed 16 February 2012.

OECD (2012b) *Education Indicators in Focus, 2012/05*, http://www.oecd.org/edu/50495363.pdf. Accessed 17 March 2015.

OECD (2014) *Education at a Glance*, http://www.slideshare.net/OECDEDU/education-at-a-glance-2014-key-findings. Accessed 19 March 2015.

Palmer, N., E. Bexley & R. James (2011) *Selection and Participation in Higher Education. University Selection in Support of Student Success and Diversity of Participation*, Centre for the Study of Higher Education, University of Melbourne. http://www.go8.edu.au/__documents/go8-policy-analysis/2011/selection_and_participation_in_higher_education.pdf. Accessed 20 March 2015.

Peach, D. (2005) 'Ensuring student success: The role of support services in improving the quality of the student learning experience', *Studies in Learning, Evaluation, Innovation and Development* 2(3): 1–15.

Pearce, J., B. Down & E. Moore (2008) 'Social class, identity and the "good" student: Negotiating university culture', *Australian Journal of Education* 52(3): 257–271.

Pew Research Center (2015) *The Rising Cost of Not Going to College*, http://www.pewsocialtrends.org/2014/02/11/the-rising-cost-of-not-going-to-college/. Accessed 19 March 2015.

Ramsden, P. (2003) *Learning to Teach in Higher Education* (second edition), Abingdon: RoutledgeFalmer.

Ranking Web (2015) *Ranking Web of Universities: New Zealand*, http://www.webometrics.info/en/oceania/New%20Zealand%20. Accessed 20 March 2015.

Read, B., L. Archer & C. Leathwood (2003) 'Challenging cultures? Student conceptions of "belonging" and "isolation" at a post-1992 university', *Studies in Higher Education* 28(3): 261–277.

Richardson, S. & A. Radloff (2014) 'Allies in learning: Critical insights into the importance of staff–student interactions in university education', *Teaching in Higher Education* 19(6): 603–615.

Roberts, S. (2011) 'Traditional practice for non-traditional students? Examining the role of pedagogy in higher education retention', *Journal of Further and Higher Education* 35(2): 183–199.

Rogers, I.H. (2012) *The Black Campus Movement: Black Students and the Racial Reconstitution of Higher Education 1965–1972*, London: Palgrave Macmillan.

Rooks, N.M. (2006) *White Money/Black Power: The Surprising History of African American Studies and the Crisis of Race in Higher Education*, Boston, MA: Beacon Press.

Schuetze, H.G. & M. Slowey (2003) 'Participation and exclusion: A comparative analysis of non-traditional students and lifelong learners in higher education', *Higher Education* 44(3–4): 309–327.

Sellar, S., T. Gale & S. Parker (2011) 'Appreciating aspirations in Australian higher education', *Cambridge Journal of Education* 41(1): 37–52.

Sheeran, Y., B.J. Brown & S. Baker (2007) 'Conflicting philosophies of inclusion: The contestation of knowledge in widening participation', *London Review of Education* 5(3): 249–263.

Sutton, P. (2014) 'A paradoxical academic identity: Fate, utopia and critical hope', *Teaching in Higher Education* 20(1): 37–47.

Tapp, J. (2014) '"I actually listened, I'm proud of myself": The effects of a participatory pedagogy on students' constructions of academic identities', *Teaching in Higher Education* 19(4): 323–335.

Teese, R. (2000) *Academic Success and Social Power*, Melbourne: Melbourne University Press.

Tight, M. (2012) 'Widening participation: A post-war scorecard', *British Journal of Educational Studies* 60(3): 211–226.

Turner, D. (2005) 'Benchmarking in universities: League tables revisited', *Oxford Review of Education* 31(3): 353–371.

U.S. Dept. of Education (2015) *New State-by-state College Attainment Numbers Show Progress Toward 2020 Goal*, https://www.ed.gov/news/press-releases/new-state-state-college-attainment-numbers-show-progress-toward-2020-goal. Accessed 18 March 2015.

Usher, A. & M. Savino (2007) 'A global survey of university ranking and league tables', *Higher Education in Europe* 32(1): 5–15.

Watt, K.M., J.J. Huerta & A. Ersan (2011) 'Identifying predictors of college success through an examination of AVID graduates' college preparatory achievements', *Journal of Hispanic Higher Education* 10(1): 20–33.

Wilkins, A. & P.J. Burke (2013) 'Widening participation in British higher education: The role of professional and social class identities and commitments', *International Journal of Lifelong Education* 30(4): 451–467.

Williams, J. (2012) *Consuming Higher Education. Why Learning Can't Be Bought*, London: Bloomsbury Academic.

Chapter 2

Teaching the taught

Whilst most people, when asked what universities are for, would reply 'teaching students', pedagogical work tends to hold an ambiguous place in contemporary universities. This chapter will explore this ambiguous place, arguing that despite its relatively low status as a means of career progression (in comparison to research), teaching can both be extremely satisfying and have a profound impact on the taught. There is a discussion of the rationale for the use of transparent pedagogies for all students, followed by some accounts provided by university teaching staff about the impact of their usage – particularly with students from non-university-going backgrounds.

What is teaching really about?

As discussed in chapter 1, the starting point for any discussion of pedagogical work is a conception of higher education as a key to a range of both social and individual benefits (Amsler 2014; Bourdieu & Passeron 1977; Bowl 2010; Bradley *et al.* 2008; Forsyth & Furlong 2003; Gale & Mills 2013; Gorard *et al.* 2006; Hughes 2015; OECD 2012; Pew Research Center 2015; Tight 2012; Williams 2012). The social benefits are huge, ranging from a more prosperous economy to greater civic engagement and a stronger democracy as a result (Collins 2013). Individuals with a tertiary education will earn more and have greater financial stability and better lifelong health outcomes, although the levels of these benefits correspond – to some extent – with an individual's sex, ethnicity and socioeconomic background (McMahon 2009; Perna 2005). It is for these reasons, amongst the others explored in chapter 1, that the higher education policies for the governments in the United Kingdom, New Zealand, the United States and Australia have been geared towards slowly but steadily increasing the proportion of their populations with degrees (Action on Access 2009; Bradley *et al.* 2008; New Zealand Ministry of Education 2014; U.S. Dept. of Education 2015).

In each country, specific demographic groups have been targeted for increased participation – largely those who tend not to have university-going cultures in their communities, and who might broadly be termed disadvantaged. The results of these policy drives can be seen in Figure 2.1, which

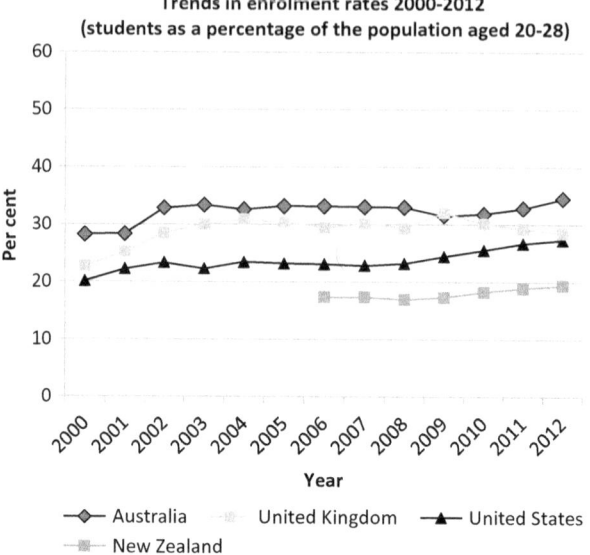

Figure 2.1 Trends in enrolment rates 2000–2012
OECD (2012)

displays students as a percentage of the population aged 20–28 between the years 2000 and 2012.

Figure 2.2 shows the proportion of the population aged between 20 and 28 years holding an undergraduate degree, again between the years 2000 and 2012, the years when the international widening participation push was at its height.

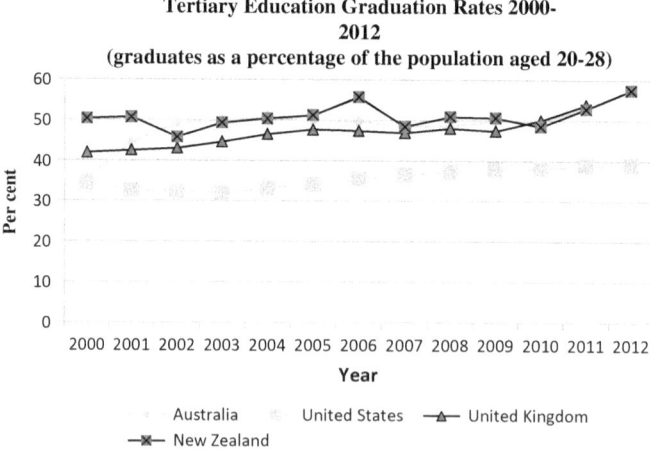

Figure 2.2 University graduation rates 2000–2012
OECD (2012)

There are a number of pressures which have arisen internationally from this increase in enrolments, and particularly the increase in enrolments of much greater numbers of students from non-university-going backgrounds. These include simply a greater volume of work for teaching staff – larger classes, more marking, more administration, more coordination (Allais 2014). In addition, there are the complex challenges found in many universities accepting high numbers of non-traditional students. These arise from their comparatively lower levels of preparedness for university-level thinking and writing, and more generally, their lower levels of educational and cultural capital (Bourdieu & Wacquant 1998; Christie *et al.* 2008; Collier & Morgan 2008; Cuseo *et al.* 2010; Devlin 2011; Gabriel 2008; Pearce *et al.* 2008; Tinto 1993).

But, let's pause to consider this proposition. It is ubiquitous in the era of widening participation to lay the blame for the transition difficulties at the feet of incoming students, or the schools they attended (Haggis 2006; Norrie 2012). This deficit model which, as we saw in chapter 1, is ubiquitous through government policy and common to the remedial approaches universities have taken to new student cohorts (Peach 2005) has been challenged:

> A transformative approach to access must stress the idea that HE should be changed to permit it to both gauge and meet the needs of under-represented groups. Rather than being predicated on deficit models of potential entrants and positioning students as lacking aspirations, information or academic preparation, transformation requires serious and far-reaching structural change, which is to be informed by under-represented groups. … Furthermore, it perceives diversity as a definite strength. Nor is the focus upon creating change via short-term, marginal projects undertaken by a few committed practitioners.
>
> (Jones & Thomas 2005: 619)

As is clear from Figures 2.1 and 2.2, although the higher education participation rates have increased substantially in the last fifteen years or so, the graduation rates have remained steady. Retention rates vary across universities, but there seems little doubt that whilst many students from non-traditional backgrounds enter universities with some trepidation and hope, they can quickly decide that higher education is not for them – or at least not at that moment, as many will later return (O'Keeffe 2013). Relatively little is known about the experiences of those who leave, although the influences on, or trigger-points for, departure are understood to some extent (Angulo-Ruiz & Pergelova 2013; Deng *et al.* 2007; Nipcon *et al.* 2006–2007; Tinto 1993; Wolf-Wendel *et al.* 2009).

Chief amongst the causes of attrition is (perhaps unsurprisingly) the student's experience – on a day-to-day level – at university. Such experiences include meeting and coming to know other students (potentially through a high-quality orientation), contact with hopefully helpful administrative staff who can problem solve and, most critically, their experiences with their lecturers and tutors. For new students who are the first in their family to go to university and are negotiating an intimidating array of administrative processes, social protocols and multiple literacies, having regular contact with their tutors and lecturers is particularly important (Nipcon *et al.* 2006–2007; Peach 2005; Richardson & Radloff 2014). It is a means of forging the sense of social connectedness and belonging which assists students to feel comfortable in seeking help when it's needed, and to persist (Devlin 2011; Murphy 2009).

Such contact involves the seemingly meaningless acknowledgement around campus, answering emails, communicating through the Learning Management System (LMS), through social media and by phone. But it is most powerfully forged, of course, in what happens in classrooms.

What happens in the classroom doesn't stay in the classroom

For all students, but for non-traditional students in particular, university classrooms are intimidating places to find oneself (Hughes 2015). Chiefly, this is because each student is uncertain about their relative comfort level, and their social location (Allen *et al.* 2008; Christie *et al.* 2008; Clegg *et al.* 2006; Collier & Morgan 2008; O'Keeffe 2013; Read *et al.* 2003). Given the traditionally racialised habitus of universities generally, students from Black and Latino cultures in the United States, Māori iwi and Pasifika communities in New Zealand, racial and ethnic minorities in the United Kingdom and Indigenous Australian students can find themselves in a marginalised space within universities. Bonds with students and staff from their own communities are vital, and strong, supporting relationships with academic staff very important indeed to their sense of belonging to what otherwise might be felt as an unwelcoming place, albeit unintentionally (Bourdieu & Passeron 1977; Bowser & Danaher 2007; Martinot 2010).

Of course there has been much written about the first year experience in higher education and how universities might best support students through the curriculum, through the use of transition pedagogies (Crosling *et al.* 2008; Gabriel 2008; Kift *et al.* 2010), and most particularly through a raft of support strategies dedicated towards 'patching' students' skill gaps, and social capital gaps, in order that they quickly become conversant with the many literacies identified by Lawrence (2005) (see chapter 1, p. 8) (Crosling *et al.* 2008; Gabriel 2008; Grace & Gravestock 2009; Murray & Klinger 2014).

Another way of approaching the question of how best one might teach diverse students (in this I include those who enter from both university-going and non-university-going backgrounds) and support those with the greatest needs is to use transparent pedagogies.

Transparent pedagogies are

- Active
- Engaging
- Innovative

- Democratic
- Student-centred
- Collaborative and
- Develop critical thinking and writing

Later in this book, there is a full suite of transparent practical strategies for classroom use which will assist you in building classroom cultures which develop all the above qualities. When done well, you will achieve higher success rates for your students, and higher satisfaction rates for yourself.

Transparent pedagogies are purposeful in nature insofar as their use at a specific teaching moment is carefully planned, with a focussed and shared learning outcome for the class in mind. Most notably, they involve the teacher being completely explicit with the students about what they are doing, why they are doing it and in evaluating each activity as a group at the conclusion of the class. Many of the pedagogies are question-based, with the teacher prompting students to think carefully about what they already know and to integrate this with their encounter with new understandings generated in class.

Perhaps one of the most critical aspects of transparent pedagogies is that they inevitably involve a shift in the relative power of the teacher and the taught. The teacher no longer relies on *connaissance* as the foundation for their pedagogical work, but rather joins the class in considering the week's material (Foucault 1991; Foucault 2005; Mavelli 2014). In this, transparent pedagogies are process-driven in a manner akin to Foucault's notion of *savoir* (Foucault 1991) discussed in chapter 1 – attention is paid to the ways in which understanding is forged, and dialogue is used rather than discussion *per se* (Senge 2010).

Teachers' talk

Pedagogies in higher education – and their efficacy in particular – have been explored elsewhere (see Cook-Sather *et al.* 2014; Fry *et al.* 2015; Barkley *et al.* 2014), yet little is known about the views of academics working in contemporary universities whilst also being committed to critical education and its potential to transform students' intellectual, social and personal lives (Amsler 2014; Canaan 2005; Gale & Mills, 2013; Haggis 2006; Roberts 2011). Below are a series of teachers' narratives about the use of such pedagogies which emerged from a two-year project in two Australian universities at the lowest end of the competitive league tables with missions to serve their local communities, and to social inclusion. Staff at these universities had high teaching loads, and both also employed very high levels of casualised staff. As discussed above, they are bronze universities with aspirations to become silver (Archer 2007; Hughes 2015).

Staff from the disciplines of Biomedicine, Communication, Creative Arts, Design, Education, Humanities, Nursing, Paramedicine and Physiology – both casuals and permanents – were invited to eight linked workshops focussing on explicit, transparent pedagogies over the course of two years ($n = 167$). The majority of the participants did not have teaching qualifications (although a few were undertaking a compulsory higher education teaching and learning qualification). Their student cohorts included large numbers of diverse, first-in-family undergraduates and increasingly their career trajectories were to be determined by data from student evaluations and student satisfaction levels (Richardson & Radloff 2014; Tangalakis *et al.* 2014).

Approximately sixty pedagogies focussing on academic literacies, critical thinking, collaborative teaching methods and community building were demonstrated to these staff, with clear explanations of their design and intent with a theoretical grounding. In so doing, the academic staff were in a permeable place of being simultaneously student and teacher. Such transparent modelling, according to Lunenberg *et al.* (2007) (which involves a focused, clear expression and verbalisation of the motivation for using each pedagogy in the context of working with diverse student cohorts), is a valuable means of assuring the participants, experiencing the pedagogies as a student, will more effectively use them as a teacher. This is brought about in professional development for teachers generally by the production of a transitory, bifurcated subjectivity where teaching staff experience what potential students are imagined to feel. This generates empathy, and such empathy, it is argued, increases the probability of participants using the pedagogies and certainly increases their aspirations and capacity to do so (Van den Bos & Brouwer 2014).

The narratives below about pedagogical work and the satisfaction which teaching students can produce were collected as part of the project's evaluation.[1] Twenty participants were given hour-long in-depth interviews. The sample was purposeful, with academics from each of the nine discipline areas, equal numbers from each of the two universities, of each sex and of both permanent and casual status. The interviews asked about their experiences of the workshops, their views about the efficacy of the pedagogies they'd engaged with, their usage of the pedagogies, any constraining factors to their usage (particularly in terms of their discipline), and the ways in which their views of themselves as teachers had changed across their careers but particularly in the light of their project participation. Finally, they were asked about their perceptions of the ways in which (if any) traditional academic power relationships were successfully breached through the use of transparent pedagogies. A thematic analytic perspective was used to explore their responses (Burman & Parker 1993).

How did these teachers perceive teaching as an activity? How did they perceive their own sense of themselves as professional teachers, despite the other demands on their time such as research and administration (if they were employed full time)? Following this discussion are their perceptions of encountering these transparent pedagogies, and their sense of the efficacy of the pedagogies in terms of building a dialogic classroom. Finally, there is a discussion of their experiences of using transparent pedagogies to purposefully build student engagement and, as a corollary, student retention and success.

Pedagogical work

As discussed earlier, most universities don't reward teaching as a valued part of an academic's workload, and are progressively diversifying the workforce with different levels of teaching load. Many are creating more teaching-only positions, and using increasing numbers of casual tutors whose employment is unstable and often unpredictable (Thornton 2014). Despite these bald facts, it is surprising to find relatively high levels of job satisfaction amongst the academics interviewed – whilst not necessarily with the unreliability of their employment, certainly with their contact with students.

Enjoyment

When asked the question of whether they enjoyed teaching, they replied:

> Maria: Love it. I love my job. I am so lucky. I get up each morning, and sometimes I want to stay in bed or I want to go to the beach, but the majority of the time I think I am so lucky in the job that I have. ... Most of these students don't believe they've got any right to be at uni, and the way our team works across the four units is that we show them very much that they have got the right to be at uni, they've got the right to achieve at uni, and it is a partnership. It's not just them by themselves doing it, it's a partnership between the teacher and them.
> (Nursing, twelve years' experience, casual tutor)

> Sofia: I like the ... I like seeing the 'Ah!' on their faces as they go 'I get that!' And I like it when they say 'Gee, you explained that really well! I was a bit confused in the lecture, but now you've explained it.' I like to try to use analogies and often in science, I relate it to food, or cooking and I love cooking myself and they go, 'Oh that makes a lot of sense, now I'll never forget how that process works.' So I like that. I really get a lot of satisfaction out of students going 'You're really good at teaching' or 'You explained that really well and now I'm never going to forget that' so, yes, I enjoy that.
> (Paramedicine, nineteen years' experience, casual tutor)

> Barbara: I love it. I love being in the class. I love the students, most of them, some of them are a pain in the neck and some of them are exhausting, but I like it when I see the light go on in them. You can see that moment where it's starting to compute, so I enjoy that. Especially if it's a topic that I really like teaching, you know? There's topics that you've got to teach that are okay but there's some topics I love teaching and they're always the best sessions. You've got to be passionate and that's the thing, the students often say to me when you look at your SETs,[2] 'She's enthusiastic about what she teaches' so if

you can instil that enthusiasm no matter how boring the topic may sound, you've got them halfway there.

(Nursing, twenty-five years' experience, senior lecturer)

Importance

The participants also held firm opinions about the purpose and importance of teaching as a means of enabling students to critically encounter, and read, their world in the ways favoured by the architects of the widening participation projects in Australia, the United Kingdom, New Zealand and the United States (Action on Access 2009; Gorard *et al.* 2006; OECD 2012). In undertaking this pedagogical work, and in using transparent pedagogies, they also argue that the material under consideration is a means of developing critical awareness in students, a lifelong disposition of enquiry:

> Q: What do you think is important about teaching?
> Josef: I think everything to be honest, I think it's the answer to everything. I think about the stupidity in the media and decisions and you watch people who have really uninformed opinions trying to argue things and the amount of ignorance around issues whether it's climate change or towards social issues or anything else. And I think university, a good education is the answer to that. I think you have to teach people how to think and how to argue and how to question and how to be creative and have fun and bring a bit more humanity into the world. I think it's hugely important, I think it's everything.
>
> (Arts, four years' experience, casual tutor)

> Mario: I don't think it's important that I teach students stuff. I don't think that's my role at all, especially in a unit like mine where content is almost secondary, but I feel like what I need to do, certainly in terms of my unit, is get them into the right habits of being students at university. I mean that's important. But more generally, I feel that I'm a bit uncomfortable with this whole vocational drive, but I feel if they forget everything that we do in class, it doesn't matter, but as long as they walk away and they question what is happening around them, I said I'll be happy. I'll feel like I've done my job as a teacher if five, six, ten years down the track they still automatically get into this habit of questioning what is happening around us.
>
> (Arts, fourteen years' experience, lecturer)

> Karen: ... in terms of accessing information students can find out a lot of information now, so I'm not the repository of knowledge, I'm not the one that brings this stuff to their attention. They'll be able to find a journal article on this if they really try. So, I think for me now, teaching is about kind of activating in them the desire to find out, the desire to learn or the desire to

apply a skill. ... teaching becomes a kind of process of individual transformation in life for me, rather than all the class understanding this or that.
(Communications, seven years' experience, casual tutor)

Power

Perhaps at the centre of the generation of classrooms in which this pedagogical work can take place, is a much less hierarchical power dynamic between students and teachers than has traditionally been in place (Amsler 2014; Bowser & Danaher 2007; Canaan 2005; Freire 2000; Gale & Mills 2013; Roberts 2011; Sutton 2014; Tapp 2014). Aside from the enactment of the foundational belief in equality which most educators both believe in and profess, there are a number of sound pedagogical reasons for teachers to purposefully build egalitarian relationships with their students. The most important of these particularly concerns students who are the first in family to attend university – less hierarchical power relationships between staff and students increase comfort levels, which in turn increase engagement, which leads to increased retention (Devlin 2011; Devlin *et al.* 2012). The following chapter offers readers a number of strategies through which to build stronger, more focussed relationships with students and, in turn, create a more engaging and dynamic classroom culture.

When asked whether the use of transparent pedagogies leads to a more egalitarian power dynamic between staff and students, Josef neatly describes a traditional academic relationship between teachers and students, and follows with the dynamic which develops when the teacher works to be quite clear about their pedagogy, their understanding and thoughts:

> Q: Do you think that using transparent pedagogies alters the power dynamic between students and you – at all?
> Josef: Interesting ... power dynamics ... I'm not sure about that. I mean I think it would in the sense that sometimes I think if you're up there, the perceived to be academic sort of person who holds all the secret knowledge and then you're imparting it to them and so there might be then this perception of you being whatever, holding secret knowledge or something. But I guess there is that sense of it being a bit more equalised if you say to them 'I'm not holding anything back, this is exactly what I'm looking at, this is what I hope for you to get out of it.' Then I guess they're very clear that we're all in this together and we know we're on the same page rather than me being some sort of holder of wisdom that may give out little crumbs or something like that, I imagine that might influence some sort of perceptions.

He goes on to describe his routine experience of teaching a tutorial simply through the use of critical questions, and the impact of this on the class. Here, he is illustrating perhaps the essence of Foucault's *savoir* – the learning occurs through its process (Foucault 1991):

I've had classes where I didn't teach anything, I just asked questions for the whole class and people are alive, loving it and pretty much that's the way. And then I walk out of it probably learning a lot more too, we've covered everything I wanted to cover and then some, just through letting them explore things themselves. It's phenomenal.

(Arts, four years' experience, casual tutor)

The high levels of student engagement depicted by Josef are echoed by Alex describing his experience of the rewards of taking the time to engender a democratic learning and teaching environment:

Alex: Yes and that's particularly, I suppose, why I enjoy it just when you're in that space, and you have that warm buzz of people just talking without self-consciousness. So, yes, when you've got past your own awkwardness about entering that space, that pretty much from the moment you walk in, they're pretty relaxed and are amiable and with that kind of sense of humility that forms within the first few weeks.

(Creative Arts, fourteen years' experience, lecturer)

David, another lecturer in Creative Arts with twelve years' teaching experience, argues that being transparent about one's teaching practice leads to a lessening of the conflict between the teacher and their students, but also facilitates a stronger engagement between students and knowledge:

Q: Do you think using transparent pedagogy, do you think it alters the power relationship between yourself as a teacher, and the taught?
David: In terms of what's happens in the classes, I think it just opens it up, allows the students in, so it's not this war between, not even you and them, between knowledge and them. It's like we're here to teach them and help them to learn and that's not just about the content, it's about the process of that. So how can you teach that without being explicit? And the cost is what? That as a teacher you somehow lose your power or control over the class? Well I think if that's a problem for you, maybe it's a deeper problem than just being explicit about how you're teaching.

Paul goes further in exploring the impact of transparent pedagogies on students, suggesting that whilst they might be unaware of their incipient influence, it empowers them to do well:

Q: It sounds, from what you're saying, the transparency of them creates a different power dynamic between you and the students. Is that right?
Paul: I think so. I think it lets them in more. I think that allows them to feel more comfortable. But also, the flip side of that is it puts more onus and responsibility on them. I'm not sure they realise that to start with. But when

you give them that idea that they've actually got control and a bit of power, they run with that and they turn in work that's just exceptional. They realise that they've actually got some control out of this and they don't just have to regurgitate what you're telling them because you're the guy that's at the front and you're getting paid to do that.

(Creative Arts, five years' experience, casual tutor)

Finally, in this section about power relationships, Barbara, an experienced Senior Lecturer in Nursing with more than twenty-five years' teaching experience and a time-consuming managerial role, suggests that the appeal of transparent pedagogies for her is precisely the more permeable power boundaries between staff and students. She argues that this generates high engagement and activity levels, even in a content-heavy discipline like Nursing:

Q: And do you think using these sorts of strategies, do you think it changes the power dynamic between the staff member and the students?
Barbara: Yes, because it's more shared, because it's more active. You're more of a facilitator absolutely because it's really about the students doing the work and not the teacher, you're just supervising really and getting them to think about things and whatever. You know, giving them instructions about the 'how to's' like 'this is what I want you to do as a group' and 'spend five minutes talking about this and put the Post-it note on the board'. No, they're not just sitting there listening to you prattle on and giving them all the answers. It's about them finding out.

Engagement

As we've seen, although teaching might be undervalued in the sector, it is engaged in by academic staff with varying levels of satisfaction (Cilliers 2010; Prosser *et al.* 2008; Woodman & Parappilly 2015). Whilst the data presented here is indicative only, given its very small sample size, there is some evidence to suggest that the staff who were taught to use transparent pedagogies, and who went on to use them, themselves re-engaged in the work of pedagogy and in their discipline. As both anecdotal accounts and the literature tell us, a strong enthusiasm for, and commitment to, subject matter are key to excellent teaching (Craft *et al.* 2014; Chappell & Craft 2011).

In this first account, Toula, a Senior Lecturer in Physiology with nineteen years' experience in tertiary teaching and Head of School, describes her observations of the changes in her staff who have transitioned to using transparent pedagogies and valued the changes which have followed:

The most powerful thing that I have seen is the engagement of the casuals and the academics who have done it. I mean, I have a difficult academic in my group who is very against everything. But … he changed his teaching method. Not great, but he did. And I think for him to change, and he's one of the more difficult people, I thought that that was a milestone. So he's actually thought about what he does and he's changed his strategy and I think that is great. And I've seen other academics, you know, the casuals just being really inspired, the new academics being really inspired. And, for me, that's the most powerful thing that I've seen, that engagement. And no matter what anybody says, I've seen it. The engagement of the casuals and the academics who have gone to the workshops is phenomenal. And I can only say that that engagement then has to reflect in the classroom.

Mike, an Associate Dean (Learning and Teaching) with twenty-one years' teaching experience, offers a pragmatic analysis of the efficacy of transparent pedagogies, arguing that they sit well with the student-centred focus of contemporary universities, but also meet the needs of a casualised teaching staff:

Q: Do you think that these transparent pedagogies are a good fit with the way that the university sector is shifting?
Mike: Absolutely, the actual pedagogies themselves are absolutely fine, they're contemporary, they focus on student engagement which is one of those big ticket items for the sector. They're the kinds of things that when I think about what are the key values of our place, in terms of flexible learning, internationalised curriculum, research-informed teaching, all of these things actually work really well, but these explicit pedagogies. Look, the simple fact is we have an increasingly sessional casualised workforce, we kind of actually need something like that.

Moving from a focus on the engagement of staff, to the engagement of students, Paul – an exemplar of the casual tutor discussed by Mike, with five years' teaching experience – points to the students' high engagement as a key, to its usefulness as a means to improve their success rates:

I think the general atmosphere of it, whatever you want to call it, is brilliant. I keep getting back to that sort of engagement word. The whole idea of letting them in to what you're actually doing, in terms of teaching, and it's not this thing that they shouldn't know about and shouldn't be a part of. That whole outlook is fantastic. It's really worked for me. As a teacher in engaging the students and getting them to do, maybe, better than they would have before.

Although the improvement in the students' grades was a less important objective of the project than was their increased engagement and therefore retention, many of the participants pointed to this as an important outcome for both themselves and their students. Here, for example, Brinji, a casual Business tutor with four years' experience, says:

So there are no pockets, there are no international students that hide in my class, everybody is fully active. In terms of success, in the study skills unit,

three students came in – what happens in the study skills unit is that students usually come in on one level and then leave on the next. So if they come in on passes they'll leave on credits. I had three girls come in on credits and left on high distinctions and that was phenomenal and I'd never been able to get anyone to achieve that.
Q: And why do you think that was?
Brinji: Because one: the transparent teaching strategies and what the sessions that we did … made me much more aware of how much more transparent I needed to be. That was one of them, and I think two: it arms students with the skills that they needed to be successful. … I think they're doing better and for some of them, even if they don't have better marks because they haven't mastered other skills, in terms of their understanding of the content and their critical thinking as a consequence of that. I think they're much better equipped.

Josef offers a detailed account of the engagement–retention–success trajectory touched on by earlier accounts by teachers using transparent pedagogies with diverse groups of students. He begins by focussing on his own levels of confidence and his commitment to the class and the students themselves:

So my experience of it, well personally I felt it gave me a greater sense of control and also confidence in knowing what to do to sort of make sure engagement is high and get good outcomes out of the students. In terms of how the students experienced it, they were incredibly engaged, motivated, you don't see people sitting around kind of just daydreaming when everyone has to stand and contribute to something and you're on a team, you know what I mean? There is that social pressure or things that maybe come alive for them. I don't know what else to say, it was just an overwhelmingly positive experience to be honest. I feel like it was amazing.

He then goes on to describe his experiences of observing the engagement–retention–success nexus as it unfolded in his classroom:

You see the reviews too … and people always said the same thing, it was always very fun and very engaging and all that kind of stuff. So obviously there's going to be more learning happening if people are engaged so there's no question they're probably getting more information and will be more interested in classes. I think attendance was very, very high as well, very high attendance and I think the social contract had a role to play. I think having engaging classes had a role to play in that as well.

And then in terms of retention, well that obviously funnelled into retention too. I mean if you've got students who are happier and feel connected to you and are doing well as well because they're actually engaged, of course they're more likely to stick around, right? I mean if you think about self-esteem, how many students come to university and feel stupid and can't cope and then drop out. ... They feel more empowered, I think they feel more part of the learning process and I think that's obviously going to impact on their self-esteem and motivation. If you feel good you're going to work harder!

Transformation

The last section of this chapter aims to complete the participants' narrative about transparent pedagogical work; how enjoyable it is, its importance and the ways in which the power differences between teachers and students are breached in order to raise engagement levels. Finally, the question of the transformative nature of this work is asked. As already discussed, policy makers and academics alike are at one in believing that higher education has a significant impact on the life chances of graduates and, importantly, that it creates more creative, logical, democratically minded citizens who participate more fully in the civic life of their communities (Amsler 2014; Bowl 2010; Bradley *et al.* 2008; Forsyth & Furlong 2003; Gale & Mills 2013; Gorard *et al.* 2006; Hughes 2015; OECD 2012; Pew Research Center 2015; Tight 2012; Williams 2012). Certainly, the data presented in Figure 2.1 and Figure 2.2, which shows relatively dramatic increases in university graduation in (in descending order) New Zealand, the United Kingdom, Australia and the United States, would suggest that these societies should be experiencing more of the social benefits which a more educated populace generates.

When discussing the changes which the participants found in their students, they commonly simultaneously touched upon some of the ways in which using transparent pedagogies also transformed themselves. They unanimously believed that the educational process itself – rather than the subject material under discussion – was pivotal to such change.

Wei, with eleven years' experience, teaches Design and sees his role as moving his students from having solely aesthetic ambitions, to using design to solve social problems – in the widest sense. He sees this standpoint as ethical:

> Again coming back to design, what I really want is coming from an ethical point of view, because I've seen through conferences and other examples how design can contribute to society. It's not just making things pretty and branding and creating want, there's a lot of areas that design could be part of, like the social side of things; environmental as much as economical and financial. So, I think ethically the reason why I'm teaching is that I want to expand that nuance, those boundaries of design from just branding, creating want, advertising, to solving needs.
>
> We try to teach empathy in a design process, which is getting away from that 1940s, 1960s designer's ego, 'I'm the designer, I know everything, I come up with the pretty thing, everyone should wear it.' We're getting away from that, so once they apply empathy in the design process they start to see that no, design is here to facilitate change. So, we've seen quite a few good students actually picked up from 'I'm here to learn Photoshop and make things pretty'

to that secondary 'I want to make change through design'. ... the first thing I tell them is that 'I'm here to ask you a question to get you confused. If you're not confused you're not doing your work.'

The usefulness of confusion as a transitional catalyst when students are undergoing change is also mentioned by Barbara, who points out her own growth points in a learning trajectory:

> Well, I still learn from students and I think teachers have to keep their minds open as well and even though I've been doing this a long time, there are still some students who surprise me and sometimes I'm wrong too. You make assumptions about students and then you think 'I was wrong about that' you know? Or they'll enlighten you about something and you think 'I've not thought about it from that way before, okay.' So it makes me reflect and from that perspective it transforms me because I think it makes me a richer person because of it. When you listen to their life stories as well it's not just about the content, it's about them – especially as course leader because you do listen to their life stories and I just sit there and I think 'Oh my God, what are you doing here?' It's transformative for the student because it could be the thing where suddenly the light comes on and it makes it clear and they can walk away with some clarity. Or I think it's successful in making them walk away feeling confused because it means they're starting to question, it's not black and white. 'There are many more angles to it, there's much more to this than I thought there was. There's lots of layers to it.' So they go away feeling a bit confused, but excited. I think that's transformative.

Maria, also an experienced, but casually employed, teacher of Nursing suggests that she feels transformed by the experience of watching understanding grow in her classrooms. But she sees the relationship between the student and the teacher, including the extra-curricular support she provides, as particularly critical to the students' persistence with their degree:

> Well, teaching can have a transformative effect on me when I see that the light bulb's come on for them. Feedback that I've had from students, but I suppose that's what really keeps you going – you can make a difference to their lives. It can be as simple as a phone call because you've noticed that they haven't done something. And, that's when you really get to know the student, and you can move someone from dropping out to really re-engaging with them again.

The purposeful development of the staff/student relationship embedded in transparent pedagogies is mentioned by a number of the participants as especially important for first-generation students. Largely, they argued that the impact on students is emotional insofar as they experience the university as cognate and encouraging. These findings are supported, of course, in the literature (see

Abbott-Chapman 2011; Allen *et al.* 2008; Ballantyne *et al.* 2009; Christie *et al.* 2008; Clegg *et al.* 2006; Devlin 2011; James *et al.* 2010; Leach 2011; Nipcon *et al.* 2006–2007; O'Keeffe 2013; Peach 2005; Read *et al.* 2003; Richardson & Radloff 2014; Schuetze & Slowey 2003; Tapp 2014).

Here, Sofia, a casual tutor of Paramedicine for nineteen years, emphasises the importance of excellent teaching, and the developing of strong, empathetic relationships with students, which she believes creates confidence in students who struggle:

> [Good teaching] gives students confidence and I think when students have confidence, they do better and I think they go on to think 'I can actually do this.' So I do think that I offer them confidence.
>
> Often I can see in their eyes that they're not getting it. I do a scan and I say 'Let's go through this again.' So I'm generally good at not giving up on students that are struggling. But I think that if they've got a good relationship with the teacher, then you can help them enormously. I know myself as a student I had some really good lecturers and still today I refer back to them, and talk about them.

Similarly, Lee, a casual tutor for nine years in Exercise Science, more directly connects improved levels of academic confidence with improved persistence and improved ambition:

> I can give you so many examples of students who often don't come in with much academic confidence at all, they've come from families with backgrounds where they're not academic backgrounds or they haven't done very well at high school and they're made to feel a bit stupid and everything else. And it's really incredible to see them with just the right sort of support and structure and guidance, watch them sometimes change and get a sense of things and see their appreciation. And it is transformative for them, I'm sure it is. So I guess it's a metacognitive thing isn't it? They kind of then have a different view of their own thinking and their own beliefs. I think their beliefs change. I think their self-esteem is impacted and their self-confidence. I'm sure they get a different sense of hope about the future as well. A lot of these students, as you would know as well, they don't probably come from amazing backgrounds or places and I think they probably see there's a brighter future – I guess if they have that feeling. I might be extending, this is what I assume to be true. ... I think it would provide them with greater hope for the future.

The impact of good teaching as a source of role modelling, and as a means of enabling students to undertake professional roles, and to have a meaningful career after graduation, is illustrated in the following by Toula:

> I think it inspires them and I've seen that. When my dad was at St Michael's Hospital, over a number of years I would go in and there would always be

nurses who came up to me and say 'I loved your lectures' and they still remember them. I mean, they've said 'I went into the Endocrinology unit because of you.' So that's my evidence that I've made a difference to the students. ... Inspiring them and contributing to what they're going to be doing in the community.

Even in the Humanities, Scott, a casual History tutor of five years who began teaching whilst completing a PhD and at the time of the interview had not secured a permanent position, also argues that there can be powerful mentoring relationships forged. Again, this relates to the earlier material about the enjoyment of teaching:

Basically I think a good teacher can shape what the student does for the rest of their life. ... I think if you have a good teacher, for example, in something like History it might make you more inclined to pursue History yourself, sort of thing. So it can build interests, it can contribute to engagement and these sorts of things. I've definitely had students that have been in my classes, and then attempted to gear their studies and career towards doing what I do – basically because they enjoy that so much.

Like Scott, Karen taught through her doctorate with the expectation that she'd get an on-going position at graduation. Instead she's taught Communications casually for seven years. Here she argues that the role of the teacher is to ignite an aspiration to learn, rather than to teach specific material. This, in turn, leads to change:

So, I think for me now, teaching is about kind of activating in them the desire to find out, the desire to learn, or the desire to apply a skill. ... Teaching becomes a kind of process of individual transformation in life for me, rather than all the class understanding this or that.

Finally, Alex, a Creative Industries lecturer with fourteen years' experience, places the above descriptions of staff/student relationships, perceptions of the importance of teaching, of the permeability of power relationships, engagement and individual change which can arise from transparent pedagogical work in the context of the institution itself. Interestingly, he likens going to university to joining a sporting team or club since they provide the resources one needs to become proficient in that sport, yet also entail the learner's desire to learn. The teacher's engagement with the students can create an environment where they feel able to become themselves engaged:

I tend to use the metaphor of a team, or a golf club, so that when you're a member of a university, you've access to a bunch of resources and people that can structure your activity over a period of time – in a way you might not be able to do in your own time. It's not so much about building the university up into anything other than just a place where you can apply yourself, and I think when you're engaging students pretty genuinely, it creates a playful place for them to learn and a safe place, so that they look forward to learning.

Conclusion

This chapter has argued that pedagogical work in higher education is an under-theorised field, and that close attention should be paid to what goes on in tertiary classrooms because this is pivotal. Aside from an academic's student evaluations which act as a quality metric for promotions and tenure, very little is known about how people teach.

Unlike the secondary school sector which has massive resources at its disposal on almost every aspect of teaching, the tertiary sector has very little indeed. For the most part, academics without teaching qualifications (the majority) tend towards replicating the ways in which they were taught at university themselves and even after academic development, they often revert to old patterns (Fink 2013). Whilst understandable, this has led to some stasis in tertiary teaching which is not well equipped to meet the challenges of the present or the future as well as it might.

These challenges include the saturation of online learning wherein as more resources are available online, the less likely it is that students will attend classes for face-to-face teaching, unless the teaching is engaging and valuable. In addition, there is the challenge of universities successfully meeting the needs of the growing numbers of undergraduate students who come from communities who have not traditionally attended university. Whilst the numbers accessing university are growing, so too are their attrition rates, with many dropping out. Some return, but many don't. The causes of this are multiple, but one factor is the relatively inhospitable nature of universities which are more comfortable when dealing with students from middle-class backgrounds who share the same values and cultural protocols.

Yet, the accounts of teaching such students discussed above, using inclusive, transparent pedagogies, tell another story. They suggest that carefully explicit pedagogical work can lead to classroom cultures which are highly engaged and can lead to significant student success. The efficacy of such practices is extremely difficult to assess given the difficulty of data gathering (the measurement of the teaching activities, difficulty in the use of control groups, for example). But it is possible to gain insight from those who have used them, and who have witnessed the impact levels.

The following four chapters introduce a range of transparent pedagogies, the rationale for their use and a step-by-step guide to using them. Beginning with the building of classroom communities which build social capital and self-confidence, there is then an exploration of using collaborative teaching methods, followed by a range of pragmatic exercises which build academic literacies and the book concludes with critical thinking – the skill which should hold students in good stead throughout their university careers and beyond.

Notes

1 Ethics approval for the project was granted by both universities.
2 SET refers to Student Evaluation of Teaching.

Bibliography

Abbott-Chapman, J. (2011) 'Making the most of the mosaic: Facilitating post-school transitions to higher education of disadvantaged students', *Australian Educational Researcher* 38(1): 57–71.
Action on Access (2009) *Mainstreaming and Sustaining Widening Participation in Institutions*, Final Report to the Higher Education Funding Council for England.
Allais, S. (2014) 'A critical perspective on large class teaching: The political economy of massification and the sociology of knowledge', *Higher Education* 67(6): 721–734.
Allen, J., S.B. Robbins, A. Casillas & I. Oh (2008) 'Third-year college retention and transfer: Effects of academic performance, motivation, and social connectedness', *Research in Higher Education* 49(7): 647–664.
Amsler, S. (2014) '"By ones and twos and tens": Pedagogies of possibility for democratising higher education', *Pedagogy, Culture and Society* 22(2): 275–294.
Angulo-Ruiz, L.F. & A. Pergelova (2013) 'The student retention puzzle revisited: The role of institutional image', *Journal of Nonprofit & Public Sector Marketing* 25(4): 334–353.
Archer, L. (2007) 'Diversity, equality and higher education: A critical reflection on the ab/uses of equity discourse within widening participation', *Teaching in Higher Education* 12(5–6): 635–653.
Ballantyne, J., T. Madden & N. Todd (2009) 'Gauging the attitudes of non-traditional students at a new campus: An Australian case study', *Journal of Higher Education Policy and Management* 31(4): 301–313.
Barkley, E.F., C.H. Major & K.P. Cross (2014) *Collaborative Learning Techniques. A Handbook for College Faculty*, San Francisco, CA: Jossey-Bass.
Bourdieu, P. & J.-C. Passeron (1977) *Reproduction in Education, Society and Culture*, London: Sage.
Bourdieu, P. & L. Wacquant (1998) *The State Nobility: Elite Schools and the Field of Power*, Cambridge: Polity Press.
Bowl, M. (2010) 'University continuing education in a neoliberal landscape: Developments in England and Aotearoa New Zealand', *International Journal of Lifelong Education* 29(6): 723–738.
Bowser, D. & P.A. Danaher (2007) 'Indigenous, pre-undergraduate and international students at Central Queensland University, Australia: Three cases of the dynamic tension between diversity and commonality', *Teaching in Higher Education* 12(5–6): 669–681.
Bradley, D., P. Noonan, H. Nugent & B. Scales (2008) *Review of Australian Higher Education, Final Report*, Canberra: Commonwealth Government.
Burman, E. & I. Parker (1993) Discourse analytical research, London: Routledge.
Canaan, J. (2005) 'Developing a pedagogy of critical hope', *Learning and Teaching in the Social Sciences* 2(3): 159–174.
Chappell, K. & A. Craft (2011) 'Creative learning conversations: Producing living dialogic spaces', *Educational Research* 53(3): 363–385.

Christie, H., L. Tett, V.E. Cree, J. Hounsell & V. McCune (2008) '"A real rollercoaster of confidence and emotions": Learning to be a university student', *Studies in Higher Education* 33(5): 567–581.
Cilliers, F. (2010) 'Impact of an educational development programme on teaching practice of academics at a research-intensive university', *International Journal for Academic Development* 15(3): 253–267.
Clegg, S., S. Bradley & K. Smith (2006) '"I've had to swallow my pride": Help seeking and self-esteem', *Higher Education Research and Development* 25(2): 101–113.
Collier, P.J. & D.L. Morgan (2008) '"Is that paper really due today?" Differences in first-generation and traditional college students' understandings of faculty expectations', *Higher Education* 55(4): 425–446.
Collins, R. (2013) 'The end of middle-class work: No more escapes', in I. Wallerstein, R. Collins, M. Mann, G. Derluguian, & C. Calhoun (eds), *Does Capitalism have a Future?* Oxford: Oxford University Press, pp. 37–70.
Cook-Sather, A., C. Bovill & P. Felten (2014) *Engaging Students as Partners in Higher Education*, San Francisco, CA: John Wiley.
Craft, A., E. Hall & R. Costello (2014) 'Passion: Engine of creative teaching in an English university?', *Thinking Skills and Creativity* 13: 91–105.
Crosling, G., L. Thomas & M. Heagney (eds) (2008) *Improving Retention in Higher Education. The Role of Teaching and Learning*, Abingdon: Routledge.
Cuseo, J.B., V.S. Fecas & A. Thompson (2010) *Thriving in College AND Beyond: Research-Based Strategies for Academic Success and Personal Development*, Dubuque, IA: Kendall Hunt Publishing.
Deng, X., Z. Lu & Z. Cao (2007) 'Attrition patterns in a diversified student body: A case study', *ERGO: The Journal of the Education Research Group of Adelaide*, 1: 15–25.
Devlin, M. (2011) 'Bridging socio-cultural incongruity: Conceptualising the success of students from low socio-economic status backgrounds in Australian higher education', *Studies in Higher Education* 38(6): 939–949.
Devlin, M., S. Kift, K. Nelson, L. Smith & J. McKay (2012) *Effective Teaching and Support of Students from Low Socioeconomic Backgrounds. Resources for Australian Higher Education*. http://www.lowses.edu.au/. Accessed 13 April 2015.
Fink, L.D. (2013). 'The current status of faculty development internationally', *International Journal for the Scholarship of Teaching and Learning* 7(2), Article 4.
Forsyth, A. & A. Furlong (2003) 'Access to higher education and disadvantaged young people', *British Educational Research Journal* 29(2): 205–225.
Foucault, M. (1991) *Remarks on Marx*, translated by J.R. Goldstein & J. Cascaito. New York: Semiotext(e).
Foucault, M. (2005) *The Hermeneutics of the Subject: Lectures at the Collège de France 1981–1982*, New York: Picador.
Freire, P. (2000) *Pedagogy of the Oppressed*, New York: Continuum.
Fry, H., S. Ketteridge & S. Marshall (eds) (2015) *A Handbook for Teaching and Learning in Higher Education: Enhancing Academic Practice* (4th ed), Abingdon: Routledge.
Gabriel, K.F. (2008) *Teaching Unprepared Students. Strategies for Promoting Success and Retention in Higher Education*, Sterling, VA: Stylus.
Gale, T. & C. Mills (2013) 'Creating spaces in higher education for marginalised Australians: Principles for socially inclusive pedagogies', *Enhancing Learning in the Social Sciences* 5(2): 7–19.

Gorard, S., E. Smith, H. May, L. Thomas, N. Adnett & K. Slack (2006) *Review of Widening Participation Research: Addressing the Barriers to Participation in Higher Education*, Bristol: Higher Education Funding Council for England.

Grace, S. & P. Gravestock (2009) *Inclusion and Diversity. Meeting the Needs of All Students*, Abingdon: Routledge.

Haggis, T. (2006) 'Pedagogies for diversity: Retaining critical challenge amidst fears of "dumbing down"', *Studies in Higher Education* 31(5): 521–535.

Hughes, K. (2015) 'The social inclusion meme in higher education: Are universities doing enough?', *International Journal of Inclusive Education* 19(3): 303–313.

Hughes, K. (forthcoming) 'Transparent pedagogies and the neoliberal episteme', *Critical Studies in Education*.

James, R., K. Krause & C. Jenkins (2010) *The First Year Experience in Australian Universities: Findings from 1994 to 2009*, Canberra: Department of Education, Employment and Workplace Relations.

Jones, R. & L. Thomas (2005) 'The 2003 UK government higher education white paper: A critical assessment of its implications for the access and widening participation agenda', *Journal of Education Policy* 20(5): 615–630.

Kift, S.M., K.J. Nelson & J.A. Clarke (2010) 'Transition pedagogy: A third generation approach to FYE: A case study of policy and practice for the higher education sector', *The International Journal of the First Year in Higher Education* 1(1): 1–20.

Lawrence, J. (2005) 'Addressing diversity in higher education: Two models for facilitating student engagement and mastery', in A. Brew & C. Asmar (eds), *Higher Education in a Changing World. Research and Development in Higher Education, 28. Proceedings of the 2005 HERDSA Annual Conference*, Sydney: University of Sydney, pp. 243–252.

Leach, L. (2011) '"I treat all students as equal": Further and higher education teachers' responses to diversity', *Journal of Further and Higher Education* 35(2): 247–263.

Lunenberg, M., F. Korthagen & A. Swennen (2007) 'The teacher educator as a role model', *Teaching and Teacher Education* 23(5): 586–601.

Mavelli, L. (2014) 'Widening participation, the instrumentalization of knowledge and the reproduction of inequality', *Teaching in Higher Education* 19(8): 860–869.

McMahon, W.W. (2009) *The Private and Social Benefits of Higher Education: Higher Learning, Greater Good*, Baltimore, MD: Johns Hopkins University Press.

Martinot, S. (2010) *The Machinery of Whiteness: Studies in the Structure of Racialization*, Philadelphia, PA: Temple University Press.

Murphy, B. (2009) 'Great expectations? Progression and achievement of less traditional entrants to higher education', *Widening Participation and Lifelong Learning* 11(2): 4–14.

Murray, N. & C.M. Klinger (eds) (2014) *Aspirations, Access and Attainment. International Perspectives on Widening Participation and an Agenda for Change*, Abingdon: Routledge.

New Zealand Ministry of Education (2014) *Tertiary Education Strategy*, http://www.education.govt.nz/ministry-of-education/overall-strategies-and-policies/tertiary-education-strategy. Accessed 13 April 2015.

Nipcon, M., L. Huser, E. Blanks, S. Sollenberger, C. Befort & S. Kurpius (2006–2007) 'The relationship of loneliness and social support with college freshmen's academic performance and persistence', *Journal of College Student Retention: Research, Theory and Practice*, 8(3): 345–358.

Norrie, J. (2012) *University standards at risk from low performing school leavers*, https://theconversation.edu.au/university-standards-at-risk-from-low-performing-school-leavers-5697. Accessed 20 March 2015.

OECD (2012) *Equity and Quality in Education. Supporting Disadvantaged Students and Schools*, http://dx.doi.org/10.1787/9789264130852-en. Accessed 16 February 2012.

O'Keeffe, P. (2013) 'A sense of belonging: Improving student retention', *College Student Journal* 47(4): 605–614.

Peach, D. (2005) 'Ensuring student success: The role of support services in improving the quality of the student learning experience', *Studies in Learning, Evaluation, Innovation and Development* 2(3): 1–15.

Pearce, J., B. Down & E. Moore (2008) 'Social class, identity and the "good" student: Negotiating university culture', *Australian Journal of Education* 52(3): 257–271.

Perna, L.W. (2005) 'The benefits of higher education: Sex, racial/ethnic and socioeconomic group differences', *The Review of Higher Education* 29(1): 23–52.

Pew Research Center (2015) *The Rising Cost of Not Going to College*, http://www.pewsocialtrends.org/2014/02/11/the-rising-cost-of-not-going-to-college/. Accessed 19 March 2015.

Prosser, M., E. Martin, K. Trigwell, P. Ramsden & H. Middleton (2008) 'University academics' experience of research and its relationship to their experience of teaching', *Instructional Science* 36(1): 3–16.

Read, B., L. Archer & C. Leathwood (2003) 'Challenging cultures? Student conceptions of "belonging" and "isolation" at a post-1992 university', *Studies in Higher Education* 28(3): 261–277.

Richardson, S. & A. Radloff (2014) 'Allies in learning: Critical insights into the importance of staff–student interactions in university education', *Teaching in Higher Education* 19(6): 603–615.

Roberts, S. (2011) 'Traditional practice for non-traditional students? Examining the role of pedagogy in higher education retention', *Journal of Further and Higher Education* 35(2): 183–199.

Schuetze, H.G. & M. Slowey (2003) 'Participation and exclusion: A comparative analysis of non-traditional students and lifelong learners in higher education', *Higher Education* 44(3–4): 309–327.

Senge, P.M. (2010) *The Fifth Discipline. The Art and Practice of the Learning Organisation*, New York: Random House.

Sutton, P. (2014) 'A paradoxical academic identity: Fate, utopia and critical hope', *Teaching in Higher Education* 20(1): 37–47.

Tangalakis, K., K. Hughes, C. Brown & K. Dickson (2014) 'The use of explicit teaching strategies for academic staff and students in science foundation subjects', *International Journal of Innovation in Science and Mathematics Education* 22(3): 42–51.

Tapp, J. (2014) '"I actually listened, I'm proud of myself": The effects of a participatory pedagogy on students' constructions of academic identities', *Teaching in Higher Education* 19(4): 323–335.

Thornton, M. (ed) (2014) *Through a Glass Darkly: The Social Sciences Look at the Neoliberal University*, Canberra: ANU Press.

Tight, M. (2012) 'Widening participation: A post-war scorecard', *British Journal of Educational Studies* 60(3): 211–226.

Tinto, V. (1993) *Leaving College: Rethinking the Causes and Cures of Student Attrition*, Chicago, IL: The University of Chicago Press.

U.S. Dept. of Education (2015) *New State-by-State College Attainment Numbers Show Progress Toward 2020 Goal*. https://www.ed.gov/news/press-releases/new-state-state-college-attainment-numbers-show-progress-toward-2020-goal. Accessed 18 March 2015.

Van den Bos, P. & J. Brouwer (2014) 'Learning to teach in higher education: How to link theory and practice', *Teaching in Higher Education* 19(7): 772–786.
Williams, J. (2012) *Consuming Higher Education. Why Learning Can't Be Bought*, London: Bloomsbury Academic.
Wolf-Wendel, L., K. Ward & J. Kinzie (2009), 'A tangled web of terms: The overlap and unique contribution of involvement, engagement and integration to understanding college student success', *Journal of College Student Development*, 50(4): 407–428.
Woodman, R.J. & M.B. Parappilly (2015) 'The effectiveness of peer review of teaching when performed between early-career academics', *Journal of University Teaching & Learning Practice* 12(1): http://ro.uow.edu.au/cgi/viewcontent.cgi?article=1505&context=jutlp. Accessed 12 March 2016.

Chapter 3

Building a dialogic classroom
Names matter

Introduction

As discussed in chapters 1 and 2, the higher education sector has changed dramatically, with a number of factors converging to create this changing environment. There is, for example, the need for more generic, critical and collaborative learning skills; the importance of formative assessment which establishes a strong feedback loop and expectations; the need to develop more flexible, independent learning environments which better prepare students for the contemporary workforce; the development of new technological possibilities for assessment; a need to respond to increased levels of plagiarism arising from access to online sources; the endeavours of academic staff to build time- and energy-efficient assessment tasks in the context of much greater class sizes; and, importantly, the more diverse learning styles and needs of contemporary students.

Many of these qualities have been formalised by universities to constitute what are termed 'graduate attributes' which they commit to equipping all their graduates with.

Broadly speaking, these refer to a general set of skills, qualities, understandings or habits of mind which the university agrees all its graduates will possess. Importantly, these qualities are in addition to the disciplinary knowledge which the graduate has, and are designed to prepare them to enter the workforce (in particular) well-primed.

They can do this with confidence given that most have also undertaken comprehensive curricula mapping and reviews in order that their particular attributes are scaffolded through each degree. Whilst there is some variation between institutions, there is a strong and almost universal agreement that all university graduates should (in no particular order):

- Be capable of effective teamwork
- Have excellent communication skills
- Be skilled and knowledgeable in their disciplines

- Be innovative and capable of critical enquiry
- Be effective global citizens.

There is debate about whether the graduate attribute movement is too vocationally oriented and skills-based (see Kalfa & Taksa 2015, for example). Others have gone further to argue that graduate attributes could, and should, be orientated towards the development of graduates with a strong ethical base, who are self-directed analytical thinkers (see Haigh & Clifford 2011; Su 2014, for example). The pedagogies set out in this book are dedicated to the development of most of the common graduate attributes – in particular, working collaboratively in groups and teams, being capable of clear, effective, self-confident communication and being highly skilled, self-directed, enquiry-based learners.

The changing demographic nature of the student body is of more concern to some universities than others, as discussed in chapter 1, yet there are a number of similarities which most students share. Foremost amongst these is their relative time poverty in comparison to earlier generations of students (Bayne 2014). Such poverty comes about largely because they are required to undertake paid work – to cover everyday living costs, but also to cover their student fees and loans (Blackwell & Pinder 2014; Breier 2010). This, not surprisingly, leads to students spending much less time on campus, typically attending only when they have a compulsory class to attend, and arranging tutorial attendance around their working hours and around family or social commitments (Archer & Hutchings 2000; Bowden & Doughney 2010; Devlin 2011; James *et al.* 2010; Reddick *et al.* 2011). Of course these demands are most acute for students who come from disadvantaged backgrounds where they may well be supporting not just themselves, but other family and friends too (Dennis *et al.* 2005). The distance travelled to campus can also be a pivotal concern of disadvantaged students since it has both time and financial implications.

The exponential growth in online learning is a response to some of the factors shaping higher education – particularly the growth in student numbers, and the financial pressures arising from reduced government funding – in addition to the enormous potential for creative, flexible learning which these new technologies offer (Garrison 2008; Norton & Campbell 2007). The sense of social isolation which online learning can generate in learners can, in turn, lead to high attrition levels (Park & Choi 2009; Street 2010). For students from disadvantaged or non-traditional backgrounds, for the reasons explored earlier, their sense of connection and affiliation to the university can be more fragile than for others, and for this reason alone, it is critical that teaching staff purposefully build such connection to themselves, but most importantly, between them and other students (Budgen *et al.* 2014). The teaching strategies found in this chapter are designed to achieve precisely this.

Whilst one might wonder at the use of the word 'teaching' when reading through the activities below, it is important to remember that before any learning and teaching can occur, the students must be engaged – allied with one another, interested in the teacher and what they have to say. This is best achieved by warming the climate in the classroom before each class begins, but especially at the very start of the teaching session in order that students come to know one another quickly, and come to understand that the classes will be active and student-centred (Allen 2008). Most of the activities use game-playing and humour which initially can feel awkward because they seem out of place in a university setting, and can disrupt student expectations to some extent. Despite this, there is little doubt that the planned, purposeful use of humour and games is extremely effective in creating a dialogic, engaged and collaborative classroom as some of the teachers described in chapter 2 (also see Antunes *et al.* 2012; Benjelloun 2009; Garner 2006; Klein 2013; Torok *et al.* 2004).

The activities are divided into three stages, which are intended to be used consecutively since they vary in the apparent level of extroversion required, and the level of personal disclosure. Stage One is a set of name-learning activities, Stage Two involves discussion of personal likes and dislikes, and invites students to share something of their lives outside campus and Stage Three, to be undertaken from a third of the way through the teaching session, facilitates stronger, more personal bonds to be formed – particularly between the students. All are designed to be undertaken in five to ten minutes – a time investment which can make a significant difference to student engagement, class quality and eventually to student retention.

Setting the scene

Building a transformative classroom begins with its first moments. Firstly, one way of reducing the levels of anxiety and stress on the part of the students is to ensure that, as they enter the classroom, there is music playing (this can be easily arranged using one of the many online music streaming services available). Secondly, as they arrive stand by the door to welcome them in. Ask their name, and introduce yourself using the nomenclature you would like them to use throughout the teaching session. Thirdly, ensure that the classroom is arranged in such a way as to easily enable group work.

Stage One activities

The aim of these activities is to ensure that students feel confident that other class members – and their teacher – know their name and something about them. This offers an immediate reduction in the sense of alienation so many students feel at first and generates a help-seeking culture and higher levels of trust. Many of these induction strategies also enable the teacher to gauge the levels of difficulty students might face, and also act as a powerful aid to recalling students' names themselves. It is suggested that at least one is used in the first class, and one each class for the following two weeks, followed by a Stage Two activity.

They vary in the level of self-exposure required, and there is no doubt that students from diverse pedagogical cultures may well have difficulty participating at first, but they are scaffolded carefully in order to steadily generate as much engagement as possible.

Most importantly, as you move through the activities, be quite explicit about your intentions. Tell the class what you are doing, and why you are doing it. At the conclusion, ask them for their feedback about the activity. How comfortable were they? Did they enjoy it? Was it worth it? Whilst these might appear to be prosaic questions, they quickly establish the high level of interaction, trust and collaboration it is so necessary to build.

1 Name Tents

Almost ubiquitous in all sorts of settings (educational and otherwise), *name tents* are a fast visual prompt for both teachers and students (see Figure 3.1). It is an excellent idea for the teacher to also participate in this activity as it provides the students with their first point of connection. The cards can be reused throughout the teaching session for increasing the numbers of names known. You will need enough index cards (approximately 130×200mm) for each member of the class, and a set of whiteboard markers.

1 Give each student a large index card and ask them to fold it in half lengthwise.
2 Ask them to write the name they would like to be called in large letters with the whiteboard markers – on both sides of the card in order that their neighbours and the teacher can easily see their name.
3 Ask them to write their discipline, major, course (whichever is the most relevant to your class) in the top left-hand corner of the card.
4 Then ask them to write the title of their favourite film in the bottom left-hand corner of the card.

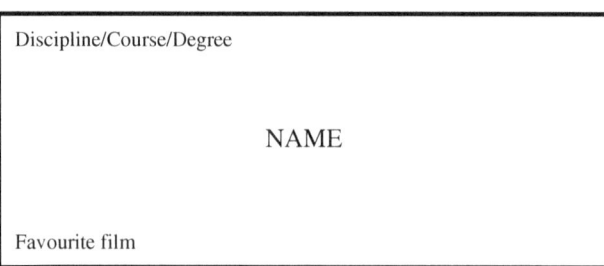

Figure 3.1 Name tent card template

There are a number of options for the last choice. You can orientate it towards your curriculum, or choose something particularly appropriate for your class. Some possibilities are:

- The story of your name
- The first song which was meaningful to you as a teenager
- Something you are really good at
- Your favourite app
- The unique thing about you
- Your favourite food
- Who was your favourite teacher – and why?
- The superpower you wish you had
- Whom you wouldn't like to be in jail with (and why)
- Something you are proud of
- Whom you admire the most – and why
- Whom you would like to spend a year on a desert island with (cannot be a family member)

5 When everyone has filled out the card (this should take around two minutes), ask them to turn to the person sitting next to them and tell them about their choice of film (or food, teacher, app, etc.). Each partner has two minutes to do this.
6 As this progresses, listen to the level of noise whilst you share your card with one of the students. Scan the room to gauge the comfort and sound level. If the levels are high, share your card with the class and then ask for a volunteer to do the same. Commonly four or five will be happy to share this. If none are, or you judge that the class is too uncomfortable to do this, then move swiftly on to another exercise.

At the end of the class, collect all the name tents, and as you greet the students at the start of their next class hand out the name tents randomly as they enter. Ask them to find the owner of the name tent. This is a fast and effective means of introducing students – and a way to very quickly flag students who haven't attended since their name tent won't be claimed.

Ask them to display their name tent in each class until you are confident that their names are known.

2 People Bingo

Another widely used group-building strategy, *People Bingo* can easily be customised to your class by selecting different statements for each cell. The purpose of this activity is chiefly the exchange of names and the exchange of low-level personal information, but also to encourage students to stand and move around the room in order that they are energised. The teacher needs to prepare the sheet for this prior to the class, and ensure that there are enough copies. Again, make sure that the purpose is shared with the class before the activity begins so that they understand your reasoning behind doing what might appear (at first glance) to be a fairly juvenile endeavour. It has a serious intent!

1   The rules of this game are that each person must find someone in the class who fits the statement in a cell, and then find others that do in order to build a row of completed cells (see Table 3.1). When creating the grid, use a range of generic statements ('I have a dog') to more specific ones ('I know some twins'). The cells can run horizontally, vertically or diagonally but must be completed with the person's name.
2   Explain that this is timed – the first person to raise their hand wins.
3   Ask the group to stand and move about the room asking the people they meet if they fit any of the cells, continuing until they have a complete row.
4   When the winner declares, read out the name in each cell and ask the person named to raise their hand. Again, this is another way of rapidly increasing name recognition.

Use variety, and statements which are appropriate for your social and cultural context. Further possibilities for inclusion could be: I swear, I like to read, my birthday is in March, I don't like pizza, I can touch my nose with my tongue, I like cooking, I go to the movies more than three times a month, I haven't read a book for at least a year, I'm new to the area, I like selfies, I have a smartphone, I dye my hair, I'm a vegetarian (or vegan), I like photography, I chew my fingernails, I don't watch TV, I have a job, I play computer games, I have children, I don't drink coffee.

Table 3.1 Example of a *People Bingo* sheet

I'm left handed Spiros	I like peanut butter	I've worked in a fast food restaurant	I've got a dog	I watch soap operas on TV
I like beer Sneja	I ride a bike	I wish I'd worked harder at school	I live in an apartment	I think tattoos are wrong
I can speak more than one language Alex	I can swim	I collect something	I know some twins	I like winter
Blue is my favourite colour Hassan	I read detective fiction	I have a grandmother	I wear nail polish	I meditate
I have indoor plants Ana	I've been to another country	I don't have a mobile (cell) phone	I like musicals	I like my hair

This should take around seven minutes to complete. It is an effective strategy and one which even introverted students can easily participate in since communication with their classmates is fast. At the end, they will know the names of at least five other students, and something interesting about them.

3 Mystery Classmate

You will need an index card for each person for this game. When you have distributed them, ask the class to write the following on their card:

1 Their name
2 Would they rather send a text or leave a voicemail?
3 Would they prefer to read the book or watch the movie?
4 Do they prefer hard copy books or eBooks?
5 What are they proud of?
6 What is one thing that makes them unique?

Give them five or so minutes to complete this, then ask them to turn to the person next to them and share their answers. If they have settled into seating patterns where they know the person next to them very well, make sure they do this with someone they haven't spoken with yet, or don't know.

Depending on your sense of their level of relaxation, you can debrief by asking for their preferences, or requesting someone volunteer information about what they are proud of, or what makes them unique.

The dichotomies on the card are of course infinitely variable. Other possibilities include:

- Whether they prefer one sport or the next (tailor this to your context)
- Do they prefer an iPhone or a smartphone – and which kind?
- Would they rather interview or be interviewed?
- Would they rather participate in an individual or a team sport?
- Do they prefer a Mac or a PC?
- On a free weekend would they prefer to go walking or to a cultural event?
- Do they prefer the mountains or the sea?
- Would they rather make a list of the things they need to do on a very busy day or just work things out as they go along?
- Would they prefer to swim in the sea or a river?

At the end of the class, collect these cards. Reading through them will quickly become an *aide-memoire* in terms of learning their names and will help in your cognisance of each student. They are also useful as a means of intervening when the class is disengaging in order to redirect their attention. In this context, simply choose someone with an interesting statement about what they are proud of, or what makes them unique, and ask them to tell the class about it. Alternatively, read the items on the card out, and ask them to guess whose card it is. Again, this facilitates higher levels of trust in the group, but can also generate self-confidence in first-in-family students who can display something of their outside lives.

4 Shoe Mountain[1]

This activity again increases name identification and, like *People Bingo*, involves students in moving around the room and sharing low-level, non-threatening, small pieces of personal information. This group builder is slightly more risky given it involves the removal of shoes, and its success level will be dependent on the group's demographics,[2] the physical ability levels in the class, their familiarity with one another and with exercises such as this. For these reasons, if this is to be used, it's suggested that it be used after the first week of classes:

1. Clear a space in the room big enough for all class members to congregate.
2. Ask them all to remove their right shoe and place it in a pile, with the class members standing around the pile.
3. Go to the pile and mix the shoes up (to ensure they don't collect their own).
4. Now ask each person to pick a shoe which is not their own.
5. When that's complete, ask them to find the owner of the shoe. This involves a judgement being made about the shoe's style, and the characteristics of the person whose shoe it is. This forges bonds of connection and recognition.
6. The owner of the shoe must then say what their name is, and tell the person who brought them the shoe why they like the shoe, where they bought it, and the reasons for buying it.
7. If it seems appropriate, and there is enough time, the class can volunteer to share the story of a shoe, making sure that the shoe owner is named. Again, this multiplies the numbers of names each student knows.

Again, this exercise should take approximately five minutes to complete. It is best undertaken when there are over ten people in the class.

5 Weird Connections

Weird Connections is best used after a week or two of classes. It is timed, fast and, like *Shoe Mountain*, is based on class mobility. In part, this is to arrest the habit of students sitting, and communicating, with few other students and encourages them to forge connections with others who might, at first appearance, seem dissimilar. This activity is not name-based but is a successful start to creating stronger class bonds.

Again, be clear and explicit with the group what you hope to accomplish with this activity – the recognition that they have things in common. Depending on the age and experience of your class, some intervention can be necessary. As they progress through the exercise, check the groups' comfort levels and if they are struggling, prompt them with benign suggestions about places they've been, films they've seen, favourite sporting teams and so forth:

1 Ask the class to get to their feet and walk around the classroom.
2 After one minute, say 'Stop!' and ask them to stand with the person closest to them and find a connection they have in common – outside campus life.
3 Give them 90 seconds to do this.
4 After 90 seconds, ask each couple to join another couple and repeat.
5 Give each group five minutes to find something all four have in common.
6 After five minutes, stop the game.
7 Ask for feedback. What did they have in common?
8 Ask them to return to their seats.

This can be a humorous and enjoyable game – often with surprising outcomes which can effectively create meaningful connections. It ensures that class members increase the reach of the people they have had contact with.

6 Data Processing

Widely used, *Data Processing* is a useful activity to start the sense of collaborative teamwork essential to many assessment tasks. It is fast to run, amusing and can be easily adapted to suit any class size or context. It can even be successfully used with very large student numbers in lecture theatres – but the higher the number of people in a group, the higher the complexity level. Groups of eight or so are ideal in terms of speed and difficulty:

1 Ask the class to break into groups. You can do this judiciously if you are interested in diversifying settled student groups by numbering the students one to eight and asking them to collect with those others with the same number.
2 Tell them the game is timed and that the winning group will be rewarded.
3 Ask them to order themselves using the 'data' of their first names. A list of names is drawn up and alphabetised.
4 When complete, the team raises their hand.
5 The team is asked to read out the names in order, and to indicate the person whose name it is.

The activity typically lasts for two to three minutes, so it can be helpful to repeat it. In doing so, again splitting the groups and creating new ones extends the students' contacts. The data to be processed can be of any variety but the following have been successfully used:

- Alphabetical by best friend's first name
- Alphabetical by favourite app

- Alphabetical by favourite food
- Alphabetical by the suburb they live in
- Alphabetical by their place of birth
- Length of hair (shortest to longest)
- Shoe size (smallest to largest)
- Date of birthday (through the year)
- Number of letters in surname
- Length of thumb (smallest to largest)

The use of physical characteristics should be used judiciously according to the levels of familiarity and comfort apparent in the class – different cultural and religious groups have protocols about touch between males and females, for example.

This exercise should take approximately five minutes.

7 Standing Order

Standing Order is a whole-group exercise involving a high level of cooperation, and multiple points of contact. Such contact can be efficacious when students connect with those who live close to them in terms of shared transportation. It can also be of wider assistance to the teacher in terms of coming to know the distance students are travelling to campus and, thereby, those who may be more vulnerable to missing classes and ultimately drop out. *Standing Order* is simple and should take approximately five minutes to complete:

1. Ask the class to stand.
2. Ask them to arrange themselves in a line according to where they live in terms of the distance from campus.
3. Using the door, ask the person who lives closest to campus to stand by the door, and the person who lives the furthest away to be at the end of the line they create. The line doesn't have to be straight.
4. Debrief with the class through walking down the line, stopping at various points and asking where they live.

As with the other Stage One group builders, be quite explicit with the group about your reasons for doing this exercise – so they know the people who live near them, so they have a better sense of their classmates, so that they appreciate the transportation difficulties students living a long way from the campus might experience.

Stage Two activities

After the completion of at least two Stage One activities, class members should know numbers of others' names, and at least one particular thing about them. It is suggested that Stage One activities are used in the first three weeks, to lessen the impact of students who arrive late and those who change groups – which commonly happens. These activities quickly acclimatise newcomers whilst also stabilising and extending the relationships of those who have attended weekly.

Stage Two activities invite the class to share more personal material. Whilst this might sound confronting, groups tend to feel comfortable undertaking the exercises having been prepared through the Stage One exercises. But there is a balance to be made between sharing such material with the entire class and just with one partner. The activities below vary in this, and the judgement of which to use can be made on the spot if it appears that the group are hesitant or uncomfortable. They are paced more slowly and are, on the whole, more reflective than Stage One activities, in order that the group begin to apply critical thinking to the matter in hand.

8 Social Contract

In the second week of classes, when names are known to some extent, it is time to build a *Social Contract* with your students. This is a powerful and critical thing to do. It is very valuable to students who are uncertain about the unwritten rules about classroom protocol, it allows one to set one's own parameters, it builds a strong sense of rapport and understanding in the class, and facilitates explicit communication (from the teacher) about the qualities the class is to develop and (most importantly) why they are to be developed – in order that there is productive, collaborative, enquiry-based learning. So begin by briefing the class on what they are about to do, and why. Building an effective social contract commonly takes about twenty minutes:

1 Firstly, ask each class member to spend two minutes writing a few sentences about the factors which they think makes a classroom feel safe. You may well have to briefly discuss what 'safe' means in this context, depending on their level of tertiary experience.
2 Ask them to turn to the person next to them, and share their answer. This allows them to test their perceptions before opening them up to the whole group, and is particularly helpful for students who are from diverse pedagogical cultures and, therefore, more challenged by democratic classrooms than others. This should take five minutes.
3 Then ask them to change partners, and working collaboratively, answer the following questions:
    - How do they want to be treated by the tutor?
    - How do they want to be treated by their classmates?
    - How do they think you want to be treated?
    - How should the class treat each other when there's conflict?
4 At this point, ask for feedback. What did they say? Frequently, students will volunteer relatively generic qualities such as 'be respectful', 'be honest' or 'be a good team player'. For the activity to be valuable, it is important to generate

more specificity so you might ask them how respect, honesty or good teamwork is enacted. What does it look like? The teacher should also be plain about their expectations – particularly their expectations about the use of technology during class time. Do you allow phone calls to be routinely received or made? Is this only permissible in a crisis after clearing it with the teacher at the beginning of the class? Are students free to use the Internet as they wish? Raise the following topics if they have not spontaneously come up – the use of sarcasm, the use of put-downs, the willingness to participate fully and be engaged in the class, the use of sexist or racist innuendo.

5 Working as a whole class, then build a social contract through students volunteering their responses to the above questions. Simply make a numbered list of statements – around eight works well. In practice, steps 4 and 5 can be done simultaneously if this seems appropriate. If not, separate them, providing time for the class to refine their responses to step 4 before moving to step 5.

6 The last stage of building the contract involves a group decision about how to deal with a situation where the contract is broken. In particular, whose responsibility is it to remind the person breaking the contract that they are doing so?

7 At this point, it is very important to gain as much consensus about the social contract as is possible. Ask the group if they can live with it, if they feel they have been understood and listened to. If there are dissenters, go over their points of contention, explaining the rationale behind the part of the contract they disagree with. Ask for feedback from the group. It is unusual for dissenters to persist once they've understood the reasons for the clauses in the contract.

8 Finally, the contract can be recorded on the whiteboard and erased, but it can also be recorded on a large piece of paper. Many using this technique ask the class to sign the paper, which adds a level of faux formality to the process and can be useful if class members later breach it – simply because they have put their signature on this agreement. Depending on the circumstances, the students can be provided with a copy of this agreement – or they can simply take a photo of the contract on their phone. Ensure that they understand the very low level of formality involved here; it is a simple class agreement, with no institutional sanctions attached. It is just a means of being explicit about agreed behaviour protocols.

9 But be prepared also to implement the contract. If it is broken, as it may well be in the early weeks of the class, be quick to point this out and draw their attention to the contract *per se* – its purpose and meaning. A social contract can be amended, so if it is broken persistently, revisit its clauses after a couple of weeks and amend the ones which are repeatedly breached if it seems clear they are unenforceable. Explore the implications of this with the group.

Whilst seemingly time-consuming, the *Social Contract* can ultimately be time-efficient since it makes explicit both your and their expectations, and establishes a formality in the classroom which later holds you in good stead. It can also quickly generate a sense of relief when the class understands the expectations, and the reasons for them. In so doing, they have a greater sense of 'fit' with the university (see Devlin 2011).

9 Using Imagery

Unlike the above text-based group builders, the following exercises use imagery and more creative techniques to generate a stronger sense of understanding amongst the class. These strategies are designed to appeal, but also push the class to think about themselves as learners, as participants in their learning but also as individuals with unique perspectives.

This exercise can be undertaken in three similar ways – through using celebrities, through using generic images or through using personal imagery. The process is the same, but the imagery used elicits different levels of connection to the images – a judgement to be made by the teacher.

1. Build a PowerPoint slide with four to six generic images of such things as animals, sports, sunsets, flowers, cars or different electronic devices – tailor the images to your group. Such imagery will lead to simple discussions of likes and dislikes, rather than anything personal.
2. Tell the class that you are going to show them some images.
3. Show the slide and give them three or so minutes to look at it.
4. Then ask them to choose one image that resonates with them, and write a very brief explanation for that choice. This allows them to practise their response, and how they might articulate their response to someone else.
5. They then share their choice with a person to their side, building rapport between the partners.
6. If it seems appropriate, and the group has a high trust and energy level, ask for feedback. Whom did they choose and why? What does this say about them?

There are three variations of this exercise which will elicit different responses, two of which are more personal. Firstly, use photographs of celebrities who have strong representative qualities – politicians, actors, sportspeople, performers of various kinds, historical figures or people who have been in controversies. Ensure that each person used represents a human quality which will be easily recognised. At stage 3 above, provide the students with three minutes to check with their neighbours who each person is – if they are unsure – then progress through the next stages. This will prompt more individual, value-based responses and possibly stronger connections between the group.

Secondly, images related to your particular discipline area, or the subject area you are teaching, can be used to help students position themselves in relation to the curriculum. For example, if you are teaching History you might select characters pertinent to what you will be teaching. Similarly, if you are teaching Literature use pictures of the author or characters in the novel or play. Scientists could use photographs of anatomy or chemistry. Social scientists might choose imagery of particularly contentious or pertinent social issues, and so forth. Ensure the class is clear that this isn't a test, simply an exercise where they select the image which resonates with them – for whatever reason.

Thirdly, use photographs which are personal to you, to whatever level you feel comfortable with. The purpose of this is to enable the students to learn more about you, to generate empathy and to facilitate a sense of commitment to you which is of assistance at the point where students are facing difficulties. Sharing something of yourself – to whatever level you feel comfortable with – can be a powerful way for students to connect with you. One very effective way to do this is to include a photo of yourself when you were at university, which most classes find both engaging and amusing. Again, use your professional judgement in your choice.

Figure 3.2 is an example of such a slide:

Figure 3.2 Example of PowerPoint slide which includes personal imagery

Ostensibly following the process through steps 1 to 6, you can conclude by volunteering what the photos mean to you – favourite places or things, pets and so forth. Commonly this generates questions which, when answered, can offer students a glimpse of your off-campus life in a similar way to which they have offered a glimpse of theirs. This can be a significant symbolic act, but it is not for everyone.

10 Unusual Questions

This is a fast-paced activity which blends innocuous personal information with potentially higher-risk material.[3] It is designed, like some of the earlier group builders, to facilitate the voluntary sharing of individual experiences and preferences. It should take approximately ten minutes to complete:

1   Tell the class you are about to provide them with a list of unusual questions, which you want them to answer on their own, and display the list. The questions are infinitely variable, but here are some suggestions:

    - If you could have a lifetime's free supply of any one food, what would it be?
    - What is the one goal you'd like to accomplish in your lifetime?
    - What are you really good at?
    - What's the weirdest thing you've ever eaten?
    - Where is your favourite place to be in summer?
    - What is your pet peeve?
    - If you had to describe yourself in three words, what would they be?
    - What is your earliest memory?
    - What makes you angry?
    - When did you last laugh?
    - What's your favourite method of transport?
    - What do you hope to be doing in five years' time?
    - What's your biggest regret?
    - Who inspired you to do well?
    - Which country would you like to move to – if money was no object?

2   Five or so questions work well in terms of time management.
3   Ask them to share two of their answers with their neighbours. Allow them to choose which neighbours to share with, and which questions they'd prefer to share. This provides a gauge to the comfort level within the room if, for example, there is a spread of non-personal and personal questions and they volunteer the non-personal answers. If this is the case, you may well consider spending more time each week building rapport in the class. Ideally, by the third or fourth week, they should feel enough comfort to share at least some of the more personal information with their neighbours – or preferably with the entire room. Equally, the questions might relate more to the course material – not as a test of knowledge, but as a point of interest. An example might be 'What is the most interesting thing you know about Chemistry, Literature, Architecture, Biomedicine, History?' Or 'What is the least important thing about Chemistry, Literature, Architecture, Biomedicine, History?' and so forth. Choose questions which suit your context, and which are light-hearted.
4   Running through the list of questions, ask for volunteers to share their responses and include some of your own if that's appropriate.

11 The Folded Line

Building on the closer rapport level touched upon in the previous activity, this one is also simple, fast and variable. Class members are connected in a relatively random manner with little or no choice, and asked to share something of themselves but with complete choice about what they share. Key to the success of this exercise is having the space to do it effectively. To this end, ensure your participants can stand comfortably in a line across the room, being careful about mobility levels. If this isn't possible, find a space outside the classroom – a wide corridor can work effectively. Without this space, the exercise can quickly become unclear to the participants.

Again, it should take in the region of seven minutes to complete.

1. Ask the class to form a line in no particular order.
2. Now, 'fold' the line by joining the ends together in order that you have a line half as long with each person facing another. In other words, the people next to one another at the middle of the line will now be facing one another.
3. When they have settled, ask each person to spend two minutes speaking to their partner about one of the topics below (which you have selected). Then reverse, so each partner has two minutes of talking time.
4. This is best done using an advice-giving format in order that there is a reciprocal problem-solving approach. After one partner has articulated their problem or difficulty, the other responds by offering advice. This protocol is a means of increasing the self-confidence of the person offering the guidance, building understanding between the partners whilst potentially problem-solving two difficulties.
5. Some suggested topics for this exercise are:
   - Their biggest fear or difficulty about their learning
   - Their biggest fear or difficulty about being at university
   - Their biggest fear or difficulty about assessment
   - The most difficult aspect of coming to campus

These are generic, and there may well be other issues more pertinent to your teaching context, in which case, use them.

Like *Zap the Problem* in chapter 5, this exercise enables students to offer one another advice, and to receive advice. In going through this process, students gain self-confidence, and potentially useful assistance with a problem. As a result, the connections between each pair grow.

Stage Three activities

Commonly, it is possible to build the foundations for a highly engaged, connected, dialogic classroom through the staged and scaffolded use of group builders from Stages One and Two. But there may be the need to include Stage Three activities which involve a higher level of personal sharing and more risk insofar as students can feel less comfortable undertaking them. The decision of whether or not to use them depends on the teacher's sense of the level of trust already evident, the cultural background of classmates, the discipline in which they are being used and the level of closeness or empathy required for that subject area, and finally they can be used if it is felt that the class requires a fillip later on in the teaching session. All three activities involve discussion of emotions (in the past and the present) which assists – in a general way – to engage the students in a sense that they are known as a whole person, rather than simply a member of a class. Like other group builders, this is mediated by the high level of choice which students can exercise in terms of what they share, and choice by the teacher about whether to ask them to speak to the whole group about their experiences and thoughts.

12 The Six Word Memoir

Using both creativity and memory, this activity can be completed a number of ways, according to the kind of students in the group. It is modest, and sometimes very powerful.

1 Ask the class to write their own memoir in six words only, using discrete words which describe their lives.
2 Tell them they have three minutes in which to do this.
3 If there is confusion about what a 'memoir' is, show them some examples of a six word memoir (these are easily available online). Even better, write one yourself and share it.
4 On completion, ask them to share their memoir with the person sitting next to them, explaining why they chose those words in particular.
5 If appropriate, ask for volunteers to share their memoir with the whole group, or ask them to share their partner's memoir (with their permission).

There are numbers of examples of such memoirs for guidance:

- Good intentions sometimes laid to rest
- Not letting go. Just adjusting grip
- Sometimes get kidnapped by afternoon naps
- Surviving selfishly. Enjoying sunshine. Needing lunch
- Loving foolishly and I don't care
- Needing summer but happily surviving winter
- Occasionally daydreaming, needing to seriously focus

There are two less demanding versions of this exercise which can be used if the language skills required for a memoir are too challenging. Both these variations should be focussed on their wider lives outside university, rather than simply their immediate feelings at the time of writing, in order to ensure that the participants learn more about each other.

Using the same pattern where students write on their own, share with a partner, and then with the whole group, ask them to:

- Write a Facebook status update for that day with ten words
- Write a tweet with 140 characters
- Write a car sticker which encapsulates their perspective on life

These variations can be useful with a less confident group, or one where there would be a lack of comfort with using the memoir format. If they are used, exemplars can be helpful, but there should be a high level of familiarity with these genres.

13 School Days

This is a lighter, less intrusive, less personal version of the next activity which invites participants to share memories of earlier educational experiences. Bear in mind that many students – particularly first-in-family students – experienced secondary school as difficult, often leaving with a sense of inadequacy and a lack of educational self-confidence. If you believe that to be the case in your class, you might choose to do this simple exercise using only their primary school experiences. Otherwise, exploring the transition to, and differences between, primary and secondary school can lead to greater self-awareness of their movement into tertiary education and the adjustments it entails. It assists students to position themselves as a lifelong learner, seeing university as a stage in that process.

Similar in tone to the *Six Word Memoir* above, this strategy requires two participants to share something of themselves with one other person. Again, it offers the opportunity to rehearse what they will share before they do it. Depending on time availability and a judgement about pacing the class according to the existing trust levels, the activity can further be shared with another couple.

Ask the class members to spend two minutes writing a paragraph about their days at school (specifying whether that includes primary, secondary or both). Emphasise that you are asking them about their experiences and feelings, rather than a simple account of where they went, what they studied and so on. Do they remember a particular teacher, for example? How did they feel on their first day? How did they feel when they left? What is their best memory of that time?

After two minutes, ask them to share this with another person. This can be done simply by suggesting they turn to the person next to them, but equally, you can group them in a couple with someone they haven't yet spoken with – it depends on the levels of familiarity and communication already in place. If you'd like them to increase, do the latter.

The final stage – again, if there is time – is to ask for general feedback. This can be a simple request for class members to give an account of their own experiences, or they can give an account of their partner's. If you have personalities which are starting to dominate or attention-seek, ask them to speak for their partner rather than themselves. Commonly the experiences which people volunteer to share are amusing. Equally, it can be powerful for the teacher to share a school experience too, since this again facilitates the building of bonds.

14 Meditation

As with all the activities covered so far, as you start this, ensure that you offer the class a clear and explicit explanation of its purpose – to acknowledge as a group that participating in education, seeing oneself as a learner, involves feelings just as much as it does the brain and the mind. Furthermore, this exercise can further the students' understanding of their own feelings of apprehension or nervousness in a tertiary setting by exploring their earlier educational experiences. It involves only thinking, speaking and listening, and should take ten to fifteen minutes to complete.

1. Ask the class to close their eyes.
2. Allow a minute or so of silence in order to allow them to settle. Depending on their levels of maturity, some students find this silence difficult at first.
3. When they have all settled, ask them to remember their first day at primary school. After a minute, prompt their thoughts with:

    - Can you remember what you were wearing?
    - What can you see?
    - What can you hear?
    - How did you feel?
    - Whom were you with?

4. Speak slowly and leave a space of about a minute between each prompt. If you feel them becoming restless, you are moving too slowly so increase the speed and shorten the pause between questions.
5. After completion, move to the second stage – their experiences at high school. For many students, and particularly those whose parents or other family members didn't attend university, their experiences in the education system in their teenaged years can be problematic. So of the three educational stages explored in this exercise, this second stage is the most likely to uncover discomfort. Using the same system of timing (one minute per prompt), ask them to think about:

    - What were they carrying?
    - What could they see as they walked towards the school gates?
    - What could they hear?

- How did they feel?
- Did they know anyone? Whom were they with?
- What was their biggest worry on their first day?

6   The last stage, perhaps unsurprisingly, concerns their first day at university. Paced similarly, ask them:

- Whom did they meet on the first day?
- How did they feel on the first day?
- Do they feel differently as they enter the university now?
- What made the difference?

7   When this is complete, give them a minute or two to recompose themselves, then ask them to turn to a partner and share with them their experiences at either primary, secondary or tertiary education. What do they remember? What do they feel about the experiences now? Give them three minutes in order to do this, then ask them to swap.

This exercise lends itself well to whole-group feedback and in doing so, it is common to find people with very similar experiences, and feelings about those experiences.

If time allows, it can be extremely productive to conclude by a short discussion of education itself, its purpose and why it generates the feelings it does. This offers the opportunity for the teacher to similarly speak of their educational path, what was easy and difficult, and how failure felt. Again, this process generally builds high levels of trust and collaboration.

15 Things Done Well

This is a relatively formal group builder, relying on a firm protocol to work well. As a facilitator, set the process out carefully and clearly. Based on groups of three, it offers the participants the opportunity to both speak about their lives outside the education system whilst also providing them with an immediate response to their experience. As an exercise, it is wholly based on positive experiences, and therefore very affirming.

1   Ask the class to write a paragraph about a positive life experience they have had. In doing so, they should be mindful that this positive experience should have three traits: it should be something they feel they did well, something that they enjoyed doing and something that made them feel proud. This experience does not have to be recent, but can come from any time in their life. The act of writing this experience down can provide a foundation for later speaking about the experience – a step which many students appreciate.

2   Give them three to four minutes to write this down. For students with low confidence levels in speaking publicly, this provides an opportunity to clarify their thoughts, and practise what they might say about their experience.

3   Then ask them to form groups of three and make a circle with their chairs so that they are facing each other. This formation is important because it increases eye contact and a sense of privacy and formality amongst the group of three.
4   One person begins and describes his/her good experience while the other group members listen carefully and take notes, listing the personal strengths that were demonstrated in the person's account of their experience. They have around two minutes to tell their story. As they proceed, take the opportunity to move around the groups, checking that people are completely comfortable and respectful. If not, intervene to keep them on topic.
5   At the conclusion, the other group members tell the speaker the character strengths they noticed in their story. Commonly, these will be such things as 'bravery', 'persistence', 'emotional strength' and so on. This is best done by the use of a key word, then offering an explanation for that word.
6   Switch speakers and repeat steps 4 and 5 until all three group members have shared.
7   At the conclusion, debrief with the class. If it seems appropriate and there is available time, people can tell their, or others' stories to the whole class. However, if it appears that the stories are too personal or too private, avoid asking for them to be aired publicly. Quite often, participants will willingly offer their experiences and if they do, their expression can be a satisfying way of concluding the exercise.

Conclusion

These activities vary in their intent but all are designed to facilitate the economical (in terms of time) building of a classroom culture which will serve as a strong foundation from which to proceed to a transformative, dialogic classroom. Whilst some might appear frivolous, others playful and the remainder very serious, they are all intended to engender a solid sense of commitment to the group, a high trust level, and lead to a strong sense of engagement. This will, in turn, lead to deeper learning, higher levels of retention and greater levels of success for students.

The activities should be used consecutively in terms of their stage – progressing through Stage One to Stage Three – since the activities at each stage have a scaffolded purpose which steadily builds the classroom community, developing the qualities students need to become successful. See Table 3.2 for a summary.

Depending on the speed of the development of your class's community, it is possible to move from Stage Three down to Stage One or Two, if that seems appropriate. Similarly, activities from Stages One and Two can be inserted throughout the teaching session simply to warm the class up at the start, or to give them a quick fillip if they are disengaging or tiring. Doing so provides a fast boost of energy.

As discussed above, these methods of teaching may well seem unorthodox, and indeed, challenge one's perception of the traditional role of a university teacher.

Table 3.2 Summary of Stage One, Two and Three community builders

Stage One	Stage Two	Stage Three
Use weeks 1–3	Use weeks 2–4	Use from week 4
Large-group activities	Large-group activities	Small-group activities
Short conversations The learning of names	Longer, more purposeful discussion in small groups with voluntary feedback	Structured, more formalised small-group discussion with voluntary feedback
Exchange of simple, non-threatening personal information (like/dislikes etc.)	Exchange of closer personal information (ambitions/personal qualities etc.)	Exchange of more private personal information about the past, consciously placing the learner in their present context
High humour levels	Harder work, lower humour levels	Self-reflective, critical thinking
High comfort levels	Moderate comfort levels	Low comfort levels
Low risk	Moderate risk	Higher risk

They may well feel awkward to do at first – although this greatly depends on the discipline in which one is working. They can be used in numerous ways to suit the teaching context and a particular teaching moment.

The following chapter develops the ideas and skills introduced here through emphasising the value of introducing – and developing – collaborative classrooms. It explores the value of using high levels of collaboration which augment the social bonds laid down through these group-building activities.

Notes

1 I'm extremely grateful to Dr Glenn Spoors for introducing me to this exercise.
2 This is an inappropriate community-building strategy for some religious and cultural groups.
3 'High risk' simply refers to the potential for students to share relatively personal material.

Bibliography

Allen, S. (2008) '"Warming" the climate for learning', *The Teaching Professor* 22(2): 1.
Antunes, M., M. Pacheco & M. Giovanela (2012) 'Design and implementation of an educational game for teaching chemistry in higher education', *Journal of Chemical Education* 89(4): 517–521.
Archer, L. & M. Hutchings (2000) '"Bettering yourself"? Discourses of risk, cost and benefit in ethnically diverse, young working-class non-participants' constructions of higher education', *British Journal of Sociology of Education* 21(4): 555–574.
Bayne, S., M. Gallagher & J. Lamb (2014) 'Being "at" university: The social topologies of distance students', *Higher Education* 67(5): 569–583.
Benjelloun, H. (2009) 'An empirical investigation of the use of humor in university classrooms', *Education, Business and Society: Contemporary Middle Eastern Issues* 2(4): 312–322.

Blackwell, E. & P.J. Pinder (2014) 'What are the motivational factors of first-generation minority college students who overcome their family histories to pursue higher education?', *College Student Journal* 48(1): 45–57.

Bowden, M.P. & J. Doughney (2010) 'Socioeconomic status, cultural diversity and the aspirations of secondary students in the western suburbs of Melbourne, Australia', *Higher Education* 51(9): 115–129.

Breier, M. (2010) 'From "financial considerations" to "poverty": Towards a reconceptualisation of the role of finances in higher education student drop out', *Higher Education* 60(6): 657–670.

Budgen, F., S.J. Main, D. Callcot & B. Hamlet (2014) 'The first year at university: Giving social capital a sporting chance', *Australian Journal of Teacher Education* 39(7): 11–24.

Dennis, J.M., J.S. Phinney & L.I. Chuateco (2005) 'The role of motivation, parental support, and peer support in the academic success of ethnic minority first-generation college students', *Journal of College Student Development* 46(3): 223–236.

Devlin, M. (2011) 'Bridging socio-cultural incongruity: Conceptualising the success of students from low socio-economic status backgrounds in Australian higher education', *Studies in Higher Education* 38(6): 939–949.

Garner, R.L. (2006) 'Humor in pedagogy: How ha-ha can lead to aha!', *College Teaching* 54(1): 177–180.

Garrison, D.R. (2008) *Blended Learning in Higher Education: Framework, Principles and Guidelines*, San Francisco, CA: Jossey Bass.

Haigh, M. & V.A. Clifford (2011) 'Integral vision: A multi-perspective approach to the recognition of graduate attributes', *Higher Education Research and Development* 30(5): 573–584.

James, R., K. Krause & C. Jenkins (2010) *The First Year Experience in Australian Universities: Findings from 1994 to 2009*, Canberra: Department of Education, Employment and Workplace Relations.

Kalfa, S. & L. Taksa (2015) 'Cultural capital in business higher education: Reconsidering the graduate attributes movement and the focus on employability', *Studies in Higher Education* 40(4): 580–595.

Klein, S.R. (2013) 'Humor in a disruptive pedagogy: Further considerations for art educators', *Art Education* 66(6): 34–39.

Norton, L. & A. Campbell (2007) *Learning, Teaching and Assessing in Higher Education: Developing Reflexive Practice*, Exeter: Learning Matters.

Park, J.H. & H.J. Choi (2009) 'Factors influencing adult learners' decision to drop out or persist in online learning', *Educational Technology & Society* 12(4): 207–217.

Reddick, R.J., A.D. Welton, D.J. Alsandor, J.L. Denyszyn & C.S. Platt (2011) 'Stories of success: High minority, high poverty public school graduate narratives on accessing higher education', *Journal of Advanced Academics* 22(4): 594–618.

Street, H. (2010) 'Factors influencing a learner's decision to drop-out or persist in higher education distance learning', *Online Journal of Distance Learning Administration*, 13(4). http://www.westga.edu/~distance/ojdla/winter134/street134.pdf. Accessed 12 March 2016.

Su, Y. (2014) 'Self-directed, genuine graduate attributes: The person-based approach', *Higher Education Research & Development* 33(6): 1208–1220.

Torok, S.E., R.F. McMorris & W.C. Lin (2004) 'Is humor an appreciated teaching tool?: Perceptions of professors' teaching styles and use of humour', *College Teaching* 52(1): 14–20.

Chapter 4

Improving academic literacies

Assessment practices in higher education settings have undergone significant change from the times when summative essays and exams were used to test students' knowledge retention. This is largely due to the changing student body, but more particularly due to changing understandings of teaching and learning, and the ways in which technologies might be employed to better meet the needs of a range of different learning styles.

The factors which have converged to create this changing environment specifically are the need for more generic, critical and collaborative learning skills (Cortez *et al.* 2009; Torenbeek *et al.* 2011); the importance of formative assessment which establishes a strong feedback loop and expectations (Baleni 2015; Moeed 2015); the need to develop more flexible, independent learning environments which better prepare students for the contemporary workforce (Leon *et al.* 2015; Monge & Frisicaro-Pawlowski 2014); the development of new technological possibilities for assessment (Edwards & Bone 2012; Johnson-Glenberg 2010; Singh & Hardaker 2014); a need to respond to increased levels of plagiarism arising from access to online sources (Holbeck *et al.* 2015; Ison 2014); the endeavours of academic staff to build time- and energy-efficient assessment tasks in the context of much greater class sizes (Carless 2015; James 2014; McCarthy 2015); and, importantly, the more diverse learning styles and needs of contemporary students (Béres 2012; Wilkinson *et al.* 2014).

This complex nexus of factors which have contributed to the changing culture of higher education assessment practices results in five key issues for assessment planning or redesign:

1 Ensuring that all students are clear about the assessment task's role and expectations – particularly those who come from other pedagogical cultures
2 Designing efficient and effective assessment for large classes
3 Using the potential of flexible, creative, engaging online assessment
4 Using assessment to develop high-level skills in purposeful and effective teamwork
5 Enabling diverse students to understand and avoid plagiarism and developing best practice assessment tasks through which to foster academic honesty

For the purposes of this book, which focuses on face-to-face rather than online pedagogies, this chapter is concentrated on the first and fourth of these points.

As discussed in chapter 1, the massification of higher education has led to both a greater diversity in the cohorts of those attending universities and demands on universities to better attend to their learning needs (Amsler 2014; Archer 2007; Bowser & Danaher 2007; Collier & Morgan 2008; Devlin 2011; Gale & Mills 2013; Haggis 2006; Murphy 2009). Universities have commonly attempted to accommodate students who are less prepared than others through a range of student-facing initiatives. Speaking broadly, some of these have included:

- Testing incoming students' literacy and/or numeracy levels and identifying those in need of study support (Read & Von Randow 2013).
- Providing online modules which teach the basics of referencing, finding journals and books, avoiding plagiarism and so forth (van Rooij & Zirkle 2016).
- Opening or expanding student support centres which offer workshops and seminars (and the like) on study skills, whilst also providing one-to-one assistance with essay writing, report writing, oral presentations and other common forms of assessment (Bukowiecki *et al.* 2009; Peach 2005).
- Establishing peer-assisted study sessions or support schemes where senior students are employed to provide assistance in specific classes, or run revision classes prior to examination time (Leidenfrost *et al.* 2014).

These are laudable strategies, but for the most part, all are extraneous to the classroom, and all focus on patching perceived gaps in students' educational capital, whilst the learning and teaching activities occurring across the university can continue uninterrupted. As discussed earlier, this institutional approach easily leads to high attrition rates of students who are not from university-going backgrounds since, despite the extra support available, they are often positioned as marginal and, in turn, feel that they are (Archer & Hutchings 2000; Christie *et al.* 2008; Clegg *et al.* 2006; Collier & Morgan 2008; Dennis *et al.* 2005; Morrison 2010; Pearce *et al.* 2008; Read *et al.* 2003; Tapp 2014).

In this chapter, there is an introduction to a range of teaching strategies which assist in the development of the many literacies students are expected to enter universities with. They are inclusive strategies insofar as they meet the needs of those both familiar and unfamiliar with tertiary literacy protocols. Through their use, the implicit is made explicit, with all students made aware of academic expectations across a number of domains. Included in this chapter are a number of strategies for explicitly teaching students how to read critically and effectively, build discipline vocabulary, write successfully to academic prompts, deliver oral presentations well and understand visual material (diagrams, images, cartoons).

Reading critically

When asked about the teaching challenges faced by academics, one of the most persistent and universal complaints is that their students don't read at all, or don't read critically, despite the strong body of literature which demonstrates that this is a crucial skill for academic success (MacMillan 2014; Pacello 2014; Rahim 2013). For the most part, face-to-face tutorials (particularly for the flipped classroom) begin with the tutor's expectation that the students have arrived having read the material, and read it well enough to be in a position to discuss it. When this isn't the case, one can be left with a void.

When selecting reading which is to be the basis for classroom discussion, particularly if the flipped classroom model is used, it is critical to purposefully consider what it is that you want your students to understand as a result of reading a particular text. How should they interact with the text? Would you like them, for example, to be in a position to summarise it? Analyse it? Evaluate it? Or simply absorb it? Interacting with the reading material through using a variety of highly engaging learning activities is pivotal to all these things.

The following teaching strategies are designed to assist with precisely this situation, but can also be used as a way to teach students how to approach complex reading on their own. They are linked to the critical thinking strategies in the next chapter, developing both students' awareness of the importance of these skills, and their ability to develop them, when this intention is explicitly conveyed to them as the purpose of these teaching activities (see Holmes *et al.* 2015).

Pre-reading

There seems little doubt that many students read rarely or reluctantly, and this may well be because they are ill at ease with both the volume and the complexity of the reading material they are required to deal with. This often contains theoretical material, and a level of scholarly discourse and vocabulary they are meeting for the first time. They often don't yet know how to approach it, how to draw meaning from it, how to talk about it or how to discuss it formally. If this is the case, the following teaching strategies are useful for lessening levels of apprehension, whilst also assisting students to link their new material with their pre-existing knowledge base. This also assists with building levels of confidence, particularly when done in collaboration with others and when it is scaffolded.

1 Learning the Language 1

The first of three scaffolded exercises, this is extremely simple and designed to create familiarity with the text, to overcome trepidation and to forge a link with the students' prior knowledge. Starting by working with a partner, it also enables students to test their ideas with one another, before they are tested before the whole group. It is premised, however, on the understanding that none of the class have come across this reading before. With this in mind, using a short piece which relates to their main reading for the week is a productive means of teaching this critical reading skill.

Ensure the whole class has the reading before them, and ask them to glance at the title, the headings, the subheadings, any images, diagrams or anything else which visually divides the text.

Then ask them to write for one minute on the following two questions:

- What do you think this reading is about?
- Why do you think we are reading it?

Then ask them to share their views with the person sitting beside them. This should take around five minutes and at the conclusion, spend another five getting their feedback. During this process, be transparent with them about your reasons for choosing that particular piece.

2 Learning the Language II

The following exercise easily flows from the first, but can equally be used on its own, depending on the needs of your particular class. The first part is almost exactly the same insofar as they are asked to glance at the title, headings, subheadings, captions, images and diagrams, but in this case, they are then asked to read the first and last paragraphs.

On their own, they are then asked to identify ten words that seem important (e.g. are essential to the topic, content vocabulary or key concepts, or are often used). After five minutes, ask them to turn to a new partner and to share their list whilst explaining, if necessary, why they think their words are important in the text. This is an important step in the development of critical thinking capacities, and in the ability to assess and argue a standpoint.

The partners now build a joint list, discarding any words which they don't agree are important and this process is repeated when each partnership joins another to make groups of four. At this point, it is likely that the groups of four will have a list of fifteen or so words.

The last stage of this exercise involves the sharing of these lists with the whole group, which is quickly done simply by asking for the lists to be read out systematically, with each group omitting words already identified, and by someone recording these on the whiteboard, on a document reader, or in any other convenient way. Inviting students to capture this list on their smartphones can be very helpful – particularly for those who are anxious about unfamiliar vocabulary.

3 Learning the Language III

Similar in tone and activity to the previous two exercises, this has an identical formation, but can be used to extend the participants' vocabulary through inviting them to think outside the text under consideration. Again, it uses collaboration, scaffolding and discussion to build a whole-group list of terms pertinent to the reading and to the topic more generally. It can be used alongside the earlier two, or as a stand-alone exercise.

Ask them to scan the title, headings, subheadings, captions, images and diagrams but then to read the first and last paragraphs (clearly, if this has been done already, this part can be omitted).

Give them a word which is pivotal to the text – using nouns is less useful than verbs given they have few synonyms.

Then ask them to spend a few moments writing as many synonyms and cognate and associated words as they can think of. If there is a sense that energy is low (particularly if this is the third such exercise they have done in the class), time them. This raises a sense of urgency and energy which increases engagement levels. Two minutes should be adequate for most students to think of at least four.

Next, pair them (asking them to compile a joint list), then ask each pair to join another and to build a combined list.

The last stage is identical to the previous two exercises, but should involve more discussion. Ask each foursome, in turn, to call out their list and write their responses – again, on a whiteboard, a PowerPoint slide, or whichever medium works. As their responses are recorded, open the discussion in order to explore whether the words are synonymous, associated or cognate, or not related at all, and explore the reasoning offered for their inclusion. Equally, these synonyms can be fed into a site which builds word clouds. If you use this method, ensure that you record each contribution given that word clouds operate using repetition, with the most frequently used word appearing as the largest.

Whilst using word clouds might sound fairly time-consuming, this can be ameliorated by generating discussion about the effectiveness of the word – as you go – whilst inserting it. Word clouds can be an extremely visually effective way to display the group's thoughts, and their use increases engagement.

These three pre-reading exercises are useful precursors to familiarise students with the text, whilst also helping them to draw on their prior knowledge of both the subject matter and the associated vocabulary. Whilst seemingly rudimentary, when handled well, they can add significantly to students' sense of comfort, and extend their critical thinking and collaboration skills. But, as with the other teaching strategies, they can be omitted if they are not suited to your purpose.

Working with text

The following activities are designed to provide students with opportunities to interact with pieces of writing – to analyse, unpack, critique and then to discuss. They are an introduction to the critical reading which is so important to success at university, but also as preparation for lifelong learning and the participation in civic life which a university education is thought to engender (Armstrong & Cairnduff 2012). They are scaffolded, but can be used as discrete activities if appropriate.

4 Marking the Text

Here students are guided to read critically through making an assessment of what they are reading, and how the reading was constructed.

Firstly, before they begin reading, ask them to number the paragraphs in the margin. The purpose of this simple act is to enable the text to be divided for discussion – if it is to form the basis for a *Socratic Seminar*, for example. If students are using electronic copies, they can do this by adding a note to the margin. Depending on the length of the piece, this should take just a minute or two.

Then, as a whole group, ensure each person has correctly numbered the paragraphs through calling out the number 'one' through to the final number. In response, the group calls out the first word in the paragraph. Commonly, there will be some disagreement about the number of paragraphs, where they begin and end and so forth. Although this method of calling out appears juvenile at first, it is a fast and efficient way to ensure that all participants can navigate their way through the text. Again, this is a space for discussion of the purpose of a paragraph, and how it is possible to identify one.

After agreement about the number, ask them to read the text and as they do, to circle the key terms and any important data and to underline the claims made by the author. The time this takes is, of course, dependent on the length of the piece. This exercise works most productively when it has a duration of around fifteen minutes. Be cautious when closing this part of the exercise since students can have very different reading speeds, particularly if they are reading in a language other than their own, and applying pressure to complete can be alienating.

On completion, pair the group, asking them to compare how they came to the decision about what was, and what wasn't important to the text's meaning. Were their results similar? Ask them to discuss why they made their decisions.

To conclude, have a general feedback discussion with the whole of the group. Each participant will have had the opportunity to test and practise their ideas, and possibly been persuaded to change their mind. As a result, they should be in a position to engage in a whole-group discussion about their views and the reasoning which led to them.

If your time is shorter than this process allows for, a collaborative exercise can be used – such as *ACAPS* (see p. 100) or the *Expert Jigsaw* (see p. 99). Both of these divide the text into chunks which can be analysed one by one in small groups and then reported systematically back to others, and then to the whole group. This can reduce the time consumed by this exercise by over fifty per cent.

5 Unpacking the Text

Similar in tone to *Marking the Text* above, this strategy is analytic as the participants look at the strategies employed by the author to mount an argument. It offers an opportunity to disassemble an argument and examine its components. In so doing, insight is gained into the act of writing itself, which can develop students' skill base quite markedly.

First ask them to divide the text into its key sections, on their own. These may well follow the extant formal structure of heading and subheadings, or not. Following the process outlined earlier, then ask them to compare with a partner and then feed back to the whole group. This is an important first step since it establishes an agreed-upon foundation for the following stages.

Again, alone, ask them to write a dot point summary of what the author is expressing in each section – what is its focus? What is its content? What did they learn in each section which was unknown? Depending upon an assessment of the engagement levels in the room, either pair them or have a combined discussion which summarises the content of each section. Documenting this visually in some way offers them the further opportunity to record a combined summary which can be useful for later revision – particularly if it is a key reading.

Having covered the content, now move on to the methods used by the author to build their argument. Using the same configuration, and a dot point summary, ask them to consider what the author is doing in each section. Are they, for example, using an anecdote? Offering evidence (convincing or otherwise)? Giving an example? Comparing their claim with others'? Commenting on the significance of their argument or evidence? Either through pairing them or, if they appear to have a high comfort level, on their own, hold a discussion on the ways in which the author chose to write this piece. More particularly, generate a group assessment of its impact and usefulness to their understanding of the topic under consideration.

6 Analysing Structure

An alternative to *Unpacking the Text*, this exercise achieves similar results in terms of familiarising students with the building blocks of a text, and with the strategies used by the writer to convince their audience of their argument. This is an important step towards being able to assess the credibility of an argument, and to evaluate the relative credibility of evidence – something which students often struggle with and which is explored in the following chapter.

This time ask the students to form groups of three, as a way in which to re-engage them. Depending on the circumstances, and their energy levels, it can be opportune to number them off if this leads to their collaboration with new partners. Once in threes, they will work as a group to:

- Establish what the author does first, second and third.
- Point out where the author shifts from one argument or idea to the next. When do they shift ground and why?
- Determine where in the text the author provides evidence.
- Decide where in the text the author provides examples.

To conclude, build a discussion around these four points, encouraging them to argue their position if there is divergence. In particular, focus on the final point and on the distinction between evidence and examples. Are they ever synonymous?

7 Approaching Writing Tasks

Whilst contemporary assessment in universities typically involves a wide and diverse range of assessment tasks designed to suit a range of learning styles and capabilities including blogs, journals, e-portfolios, oral presentations, research projects and so forth, all have one thing in common: the question to be answered. Of course these will vary in complexity in terms of Bloom's revised taxonomy and depending on whether they are used as formative or summative (Krathwohl 2002). Commonly – particularly in their first year – students are unclear precisely what they are being asked to do, and so either miss the question or don't provide a comprehensive answer. In the following chapter there is a comprehensive discussion of Bloom, and the ways in which questions might be productively built and utilised as a teaching tool.

Becoming familiar, then, with the expectations of answering questions begins with an understanding of the implicit structure within the questions and this hinges on the words used. It is worth spending time, either in class or online if it includes blended learning, offering students some tools through which to understand expectations.

In the first instance, provide each person in the group with either one, or a number of questions which they may choose from which have varied key (instructive) words drawn from the list on p. 76.

Using the same configuration as above (working initially on their own, then with a partner and finally with the whole group), ask them to consider the following:

- What am I supposed to do as a writer when I respond to this?
- What am I expected to cover in this piece of writing?
- From which perspective am I being asked to write?
- Who is my audience?
- What type of text am I being asked to write? What do I know about this genre?
- Does this question ask me to use resources? If so, what resources should I use?
- Does the question tell me to focus on a specific text?
- Are there clues in the question that will help me organise my paper?

When the group has formed a collective view of the answers to these questions, move to the next exercise, if it appears that they are under-confident – particularly about the final point above. All questions contain clues to assist in organising an answer. The important thing is to know what they are.

8 Analysing Questions

Use this strategy once, at the most, if it appears necessary from the students' lack of clarity or certainty about the writing task they are to undertake. If they've had the experience of the exercises earlier in this chapter, they should be in a position to critically analyse the language embedded in the question relatively easily.

Split the class into four groups, and provide each group with a list of words which are pertinent to your discipline and appear in the questions they are asked to respond to. The following examples are used commonly in arts and humanities, for example:

Group One: Analyse; assess; compare and contrast; critique
Group Two: Define; describe; discuss; evaluate
Group Three: Explain; identify; illustrate; interpret
Group Four: Justify; outline; respond, summarise

These group sizes can be simply changed if time is an issue with an eight-group formation considering two words each, for example.

Ask them to define their words together in (about) five minutes and to appoint a spokesperson who then reads their definitions to the whole class who, in turn, come to a group understanding of the definitions. Unlike the earlier teaching strategies where no exemplar is offered, it can be worthwhile in this context to offer one since clarity about the requirements of the assessment task is key to the ability to complete it successfully. Explain this clearly if you decide to offer an exemplar, in order to emphasise that the key words do have context-specific meaning which will be influential both in the structuring and shaping of their writing, and most importantly in the way in which it is assessed.

Table 4.1 offers a suggested list of the terms above, with their commonly understood meaning, but, again, adjust to your discipline and the style of questions used.

A further step can be taken if the group needs to practise the analysis of writing prompts.

Firstly break them into groups of four and provide each group with a typical essay question – this can be aligned with your discipline or a cognate discipline or even from another discipline area entirely. The purpose is to analyse a question (rather than to answer it) and to propose a way in which to structure a potential answer.

Table 4.1 Definitions of commonly used writing prompts

Analyse	Break the object of enquiry into parts, explain them and how they relate to each other
Assess	Make a judgement about the value of something (often in relation to something else)
Compare and contrast	Discuss the similarities and differences between two things
Critique	Discuss the negative elements of the object of enquiry and provide evidence to justify your position
Define	Provide the meaning for a term in enough detail to show that you fully understand what it means
Describe	Use 'how', 'where', 'who' and 'why' to build a complete picture of the idea, place, person, theory or thing
Discuss	Explore the topic from different perspectives, including its advantages and disadvantages
Evaluate	Using evidence, discuss the strengths and weaknesses
Explain	Provide a detailed account of the topic, then the reasons for its existence or meaning
Identify	List and explain
Illustrate	Provide examples of the topic, and show the links between the topic and examples
Interpret	Provide the meaning of something, using examples to make the point clear
Justify	Give the reasons for a claim
Outline	Make a logical listing of the important points of a topic
Relate	Show the connections between things, or show how one thing causes another
Respond	State your overall response to the topic or idea and then explain your response using specific examples
Summarise	Bring together and articulate the main points of something – without your responses to it. Write in a structured way (with main points and sub-points)

The following list offers examples from the Arts and Humanities which can be used for this exercise, if appropriate:

- Piaget and Vygotsky are both constructivists. They share several similar ideas about how children learn. However, they do disagree on several points about cognitive development. Discuss one way in which Piaget and Vygotsky share similar ideas, and discuss one way in which their views differ.
- Evaluate the arguments made that we need a universal healthcare system.

- In the past forty years, divorce rates have risen steadily in Western societies. Identify the reasons for this increase, and describe its impact on society generally.
- Illustrate the way in which schools could make the best use of information technology in the classroom.
- Compare and contrast the central themes in the work of Charles Dickens and Thomas Hardy.
- Analyse the origins of the Second World War. To what extent could it have been avoided?
- 'A nation's greatness is measured by how it treats its weakest members' (Mahatma Ghandi). Relate this statement to contemporary society, and make an assessment of our society's greatness.

Ask each group of four to identify the key word(s) in the essay title which will determine how they will organise their response. Then ask them to map out what the macrostructure of the essay would look like, and what resources they would draw on to provide the evidence they would need in order to answer it successfully.

This should take approximately twenty minutes to complete. Conclude with each group sharing their approach to the question with the whole group. In this way, each participant can access more than simply their own response and become more familiar with the ways in which key words direct the essay's structure.

Again, this is a relatively rudimentary exercise to be used only where there is a strong need. Most universities' learning and teaching centres hold online resources very similar in format to the above and students should be encouraged to make full use of them. If, however, they don't use available resources, or are unclear about essay structures or those of other writing tasks, this exercise can be of assistance. It can equally be adapted for numbers of different contexts.

The following six activities are similarly orientated towards offering students a set of fundamental tools of exploration, which should equip them to critically approach different objects of analysis. They are very similar in nature using collaboration, examination, assessment and evaluation.

Critical analysis

9 Analysing Photographs

As discussed in chapter 3, the use of images can be a powerful way to engage students in a topic or as a catalyst which helps to generate discussion and collaboration, particularly if one's feelings are engaged by the image. Bachleitner & Weichbold (2015) argue that there is a three-step process involved in the contemplation of an image: the first is the pure visual impact of the image; the second stage involves its consideration and a cognitive engagement; the final part occurs when there is a conversion of the image's meaning (or rather the viewer's perception of its meaning) into words. Images, then, can be a rich and valuable resource to draw on, particularly when students are given a framework within which to undertake the third step of this process.

This exercise has similarities with *ACAPS* which is discussed in chapter 5 insofar as a photograph can as easily be used for that activity as text can be, and it also contains an analytical framework. Here, however, the class is asked to undertake a more detailed analysis of the image and its meaning. In doing so, the use of smartphones or tablets is beneficial since it facilitates the addition of further information to contextualise the image more fully.

A simple group formation and feedback protocol should be used for this since it is a collaborative activity focussed on an object initially, and then should move to a whole-group discussion. Divide the tutorial into groups of two, three or four – whichever size suits your needs. Ask each group to answer the following questions which fall under three broad rubrics:

Identify the photograph

- Who took it?
- When did they take it?
- Why did they take it?
- Whom was it for?

Examine the photograph

- Explain what is happening in the photograph – the subject and scene.
- Divide the photograph into four, and examine each part separately – the individuals depicted, the objects present, the background and anything else of interest.
- Which part of the photograph is the most important in enabling its analysis?

Evaluate the photograph

- How accurate a portrayal is the photograph?
- What is it missing?
- What was the photographer trying to achieve by taking this particular shot?
- What questions remain about the photograph?

Commonly the analysis takes about twenty minutes and the following discussion around the same amount of time, but this depends on the complexity of the photograph (particularly how well known it is). In choosing a specific photograph for this exercise, it is advantageous to select one which has both a sense of familiarity and the unexpected, but which is not very well known. At the conclusion of the exercise, the students should be in a position to 'read' imagery, looking for, and assessing, indications of its meaning.

10 Analysing Artefacts

The term *artefact* is used loosely here to refer to any tactile object of enquiry. Dependent on which discipline is being taught, these can vary from items of fashion, to items from the past, curios, letters, household objects – any number of miscellaneous materials which suit the teaching moment and, particularly, which are likely to excite curiosity about the item's origins, design and purpose (see Guyver 2012; Radford 2014; Ryan & Brough 2012).

Again, the purpose of this teaching activity is not only to engage interest, but to provide students with a set of tools through which to approach an artefact, to be able to read clues and to draw on prior knowledge in order to analyse it. Artefacts, then, can be used as a catalyst for stimulating interest in a topic in a similar way to photographs in the previous exercise.

The configuration is identical – small groups of a suitable number working on a sequence of questions and their responses to the questions (including the thought processes which led to the answers) being reported to the whole group and discussed.

The following questions are relatively generic in nature and can be varied and altered for different purposes and artefacts:

- What kind of artefact is this? What is it?
- At what time was it created?
- What is (was) its purpose?
- What do the artefact's qualities suggest about the period it was created? Consider the materials used in its manufacture, any evident text or markings, its colour and shape.
- Does the artefact have any significance?
- Can other inferences be drawn from it?
- What questions might be asked of the creator or manufacturer of the artefact?

11 Analysing Graphs

The ability to confidently read data reported in graphs can be a key skill missing for many undergraduates, yet an important one to learn if they are in any discipline which uses data – which they all do to varying extents. This exercise is about teaching students how to 'read' something other than text, how to assess it and how to analyse it. It's a useful tool for use as a scaffolding method in order that they can build their skills in approaching data before they are presented with statistics in the course material itself.

A compelling motivation for using this teaching strategy (aside from the pragmatic need to improve students' ability to read and understand data) is that it can improve their familiarity with, and confidence in, numeracy. There is a broad international literature which argues that undergraduates not enrolled in Science, Technology,

Engineering or Mathematics (STEM) are commonly lacking in numerical literacy and, critically, have a generalised lack of confidence and even a level of anxiety about their numeracy levels (see Chamberlain *et al.* 2015; Tariq & Durrani 2012; Tariq *et al.* 2013). The following exercise, then, is an accessible introduction to building confidence and numeracy at a relatively basic level. There is a degree of collaboration involved which can be useful when there are different levels of numerical literacy in the room.

Perhaps the most important part of this exercise is to select an appropriate graph to analyse – it should be on topic, challenging, but not so complex that the participants in the class will struggle to follow it. Using longitudinal data, for example, allows for the appreciation of the data levels, but adds the layer of change over time, and then asks for an accounting for that change.

One possibility for this exercise is to split the group into threes or fours, otherwise it can be undertaken as a whole-group exercise with the tutor stepping the class through each stage. If the group is very under-confident, the whole-group approach is recommended.

Show them the graph. This is best done in a way which enables close scrutiny rather than displayed on a large screen, simply because when working on it, the small group can point to its specific components. The following questions are general in nature and can, of course, be altered to suit the teaching moment. They guide the students to a reading of the graph in a manner not unlike the reading of a photograph, artefact or piece of writing:

- Ask them to record the title of the graph.
- Next, ask them to locate the source of the data presented.
- How credible is that source? Did it originate in a university, for example? Was it produced by an arm of government?
- Ask them to record the headings on the X and Y axes. Precisely what is being reported and why?
- Ask them to read the labels under each column. Are any subgroups being compared?
- What can one learn from comparing one column to the next?
- What can be inferred from the graph?
- Ask them to write a summary – in two minutes – of what they learned from the graph.
- Finally, as a general point of discussion, ask them to consider if anything is missing from the graph which would assist in building a more comprehensive picture of their topic.

This final stage enables a critical approach towards the graph to be built insofar as it involves the theoretical extension of the data presented and, in turn, facilitates the students' sense of mastery over the material. It is, therefore, well worth the time spent.

12 Analysing Sound Recordings

Audio recordings can be used as objects for analysis in similar ways to the artefacts, photographs and graphs discussed above. There is a body of literature which explores the use of sound in disciplines such as Psychology (Rush 2014), Creative Arts (Claydon 2007), Physics (Özkan & Selçuk 2013), Design (Tahiroğlu *et al.* 2014) and Creative Writing (Ahern 2013) amongst others, but in the main, sound is used as a means to consider something else. In the Arts, Humanities and Social Sciences, in particular, audio recordings of public speeches, music or even atmospheric sounds can be useful materials for initiating an exploration of numbers of topics. If sound recordings are to be used, ensure that they are relatively easily recognised or relatively easily analysed, and are of no more than five to ten minutes' duration.

This is a collaborative learning method which can be structured to suit. The possibilities are:

- Undertaking it as a whole group
- Asking students to work in pairs, with feedback
- Asking students to work in pairs, then fours, with feedback
- Using the *Expert Jigsaw* method (see p. 99)

Whichever formation is chosen, use the following questions to assist in shaping the discussion, leaving the final question for consideration by the whole group:

- What kind of a recording is this? (Commercially produced? A public broadcast? A political speech? Informally recorded? A vox pop?)
- At what point in time was the recording made? How can this be determined? In what social context was the recording made?
- For whom was the recording produced?
- What was the purpose of the recording? Why was it recorded?
- Are there emotions embedded in the recording? If so, what are they?
- Is the recording designed to generate emotions in its audience? If so, what are they?
- What remaining questions are there about this recording?

13 Assessing Academic Credibility

Alongside the dramatic structural changes which have occurred across the higher education sector over the past twenty years which were detailed earlier, there has been a massive increase in the use of online teaching tools through formal Learning Management System (LMS) platforms which determine the ways in which material is delivered to students, and the patterns of staff–student, student–staff and student–student interactions. In particular, this has meant adopting a range of different social media tools that attempt to meet the diverse and shifting landscape of education in the twenty-first century (Losh 2014).

Online fora of various kinds create national and global communities of practice, and facilitate, it could be argued, the democratisation of research and information. They also broaden the reach of research, make it instantaneous and interactive, and centralise it as a tool of student learning. One of the challenges here, however, is developing students' ability to make a distinction between credible and incredible sources of the material available online (see Greenberg et al. 2013; Subramaniam et al. 2015). Indeed, there is a literature which argues that the role of contemporary academics is to teach students to think and to problem-solve effectively, rather than to teach them discrete bodies of knowledge (of course the strength of this argument varies according to discipline area; one would like medical students to understand the mechanics of the body, for example) (Holmes et al. 2015).

An example of this process in train is provided by the analogy of London's taxi drivers who, until recently, spent at least two years on a scooter learning each and every street in the London metropolitan region. Today, none of this time, energy or memory is necessary as we have Global Positioning Systems where any destination can be found in seconds and the fastest route there displayed for the cab driver, including the levels of traffic on a number of possible routes. In essence, one doesn't need to know things – all one needs to know is how to undertake effective research, and how to make a reliable assessment of a source's credibility. This can be perplexing for many undergraduates.

The volume of information and number of data sources have grown exponentially over the past twenty years. Perhaps unsurprisingly, this is largely because of our ability to reproduce text quickly and cheaply, and to send it or post it immediately. Similarly, it can be argued that the traditional gatekeepers to publication (publishing companies, newspaper editors, peer-reviewed journal editors and so forth) who check for credibility and quality have been undermined. This has been undertaken by predatory media and publishing businesses which, whilst purporting to carry credibility, in fact have none, given that they do not review in any meaningful way (if at all) and may even ask authors to pay a publication fee (Beall 2015; Carmichael & MacMillan 2011; Cooper 2013; Garz et al. 2015; McCabe & Snyder 2014; Valanto et al. 2015).

Similarly, improved technology has meant that it has become much easier and cheaper for books to be published. Established, reputable publishing houses still exert robust quality control over their authors and their publications, but there are numerous vanity publishers willing to publish without any meaningful quality control beyond ensuring the manuscript is legally sound. Equally, one can self-publish with little effort (see Carolan & Evain 2013; Hall 2013).

Aside from these changes to scholarly sources, there has also been a huge growth in the numbers of websites – some reliable and trustworthy, others compiled by individuals who may well consider themselves an expert on a topic and claim that they are, when in fact, they have no academic qualifications in the field they are writing about (see Charbonneau 2015; Go et al. 2016). Clearly, such individuals often align themselves with causes or topics which are socially contentious and seek to bolster an unusual position with material which is seemingly credible but, again, is not (see Connelly *et al.* 2016; Dunbar 2014).

In this resource-rich environment, many undergraduates find it extremely difficult to make a judgement about which sources – amongst the many – are reasonable, or acceptable, to use as evidence for academic work. Wikipedia is perhaps the most disputed yet widely used information source by the general public – and by students and academics. Whether it is a reasonable resource for use in assessment tasks is contentious and an issue which should be openly discussed with students from the outset (see Bilić 2015; Leitch 2014; O'Sullivan 2009; Schroeder & Taylor 2015). Depending on the discipline, it is also useful to be precise about which style of writing is acceptable in an academic context – blogs? Facebook pages? Tweets? Self-published books? Vanity-published books? Newspaper articles and so forth?

Here, then, it is worth developing students' ability to discern online credibility and the following exercise, which has a similar pattern to those above, provides students with an enquiry-based framework through which to make such an assessment. It should help students think critically – and analytically – about what they read online through answering a set of structured, sequential questions which will help students interrogate websites, in particular, but can easily be used for other online fora. In doing so, encourage them to use whatever is at hand to undertake the background research.

The best kind of website to select for this exercise is one which purports to be reliable but is, in fact, attempting to sway its audience towards its point of view through the use of strong imagery, polemic language or specious arguments. A website which also draws on unreliable data from insubstantial sources provides even more material to analyse. Ideally, the website in question will be screened in the room, whilst the class also have the tools to scrutinise it more closely in their seats.

Using one of the classroom formations described in *Analysing Sound Recordings*, ask the group to cover the following set of questions:

- What is the title of the website? Is it an acronym? If it is, why is the acronym used?
- Who is the website's author – in other words, who lays claim to it? What can be found about the author's background and credentials? If it is anonymous, who might be the author?
- What purpose does the website serve? Whom is it for?
- What claims does the website make?
- Do you sense bias? If so, what specific language indicates that this might not be an indifferent website?
- Are the author's sources credible? What makes you think that?
- Is the website convincing to you? Why or why not?

Again, it is useful to draw the group together at the end in order to answer the final question: What questions remain for you about this website? This facilitates both a useful conclusion, but also a means for the participants to think more widely about credibility, and the ways in which as developing writers themselves, they might better increase their own academic credibility through a careful use of references and information sources.

In whichever format *Assessing Academic Credibility* is used, it will make an economical and explicit contribution to reasoning ability and standpoint development amongst first-year undergraduates. In doing so, it will help to cultivate the habits of mind (Costa & Kallick 2008) which encourage and support students to become judicious, thinking critically about the credibility of what they watch and read.

Developing oral fluency

Whilst student presentations are ubiquitous in tertiary education given that fluent oral communication skills are perceived as a key graduate attribute, they can be problematic for a number of reasons: they can generate a good deal of anxiety (Turner *et al.* 2013), there can be gender differences in students' approach to (and success in) oral presentations (Bhati 2012) and they can be complex to assess well given there are both content and delivery to consider (see Aryadoust 2015; García-Ros 2011; Turner *et al.* 2013; van Ginkel *et al.* 2015). They can also commonly lead to a relatively uninteresting block of time for the non-presenters if they are delivered in class, which has led to presentation innovations involving video-recorded presentations (see Murphy & Barry 2016).

The final two teaching strategies in this chapter are, again, to be used judiciously with groups whose assessment includes an oral presentation and whose presentation skills might be under-developed for the task. In particular, they are designed to build confidence, to assist students to become familiar with public presentations and to improve their ability to operate under some stress.

14 Two-minute speeches

The simplest of teaching strategies, this can take as much or as little time as seems appropriate. Whilst also an amusing activity, there is a judgement to be made about whether or not to ask each class member to deliver their two-minute speech, whether to ask for volunteers or whether to request that particular students give their speech. The latter is useful if there is the time, given students will learn much from one another's presentations, and it means that the students more in need of the activity will engage with it. Similarly, the choice can be made of whether to provide them with a selection of on-topic or with not-on-topic prompts (a mixture of the two provides variety and amusement). When writing on-topic prompts, ensure that they are simple and short, given that the students will have a very short amount of preparation time in order to put them under a little pressure.

The following are examples of not-on-topic prompts which can readily be used for this exercise:

- Tattoos are like getting a bad haircut which you will never be able to get rid of
- Trees make people happy
- Every child should learn a musical instrument
- (Celebrity's name) should retire
- Apostrophes should be banned
- Apple is better than Microsoft
- 50 is the new 20
- Social media means we don't need friends anymore
- We should drink more alcohol as it makes life fun, and life is all about fun
- Teenagers are wonderful. We should embrace them as a community

Once you have a prompt for each member of the group, place the prompts in a receptacle and ask each individual to pick one, without looking at it. Alternatively, you can hand them out either purposefully or randomly, depending on the teaching context.

Provide them with five minutes' preparation time, inviting them to use the Internet for any evidence which bolsters their argument. Ensure that they are aware that they must be in a position to speak on their topic for two minutes.

Depending on the numbers in the room, and the time allocated to this, the class members deliver their speeches one after the other in quick succession. It can be helpful to use a stopwatch to time each presentation, to give them a one minute warning, a thirty second warning and to simply terminate them if they go over two minutes.

This is a simple, fast-paced exercise which, whilst appearing light-hearted, also has a serious intent and it can be extremely effective at building self-confidence levels. If a safe, dialogic culture has been built in the class through the use of the teaching strategies outlined in chapter 3, students should feel assured that they will be supported when giving their two-minute speech.

15 Speakers' Panel

This activity works well alongside others (such as the *Socratic Seminar*), using related conventions such as one person representing and expressing the views of a small group. Also similar in tone, a speakers' panel has a relatively high formality level, and clear protocols. It gives students the opportunity to practise speaking in front of an audience, to listen effectively and to develop higher-level questions to advance communication and deepen learning. It is best used with a thought-provoking text on which to base the discussion, and with an attached question which is likely to promote vigorous debate.

Such a panel can be assembled after some preparatory work on the text using, for example, *ACAPS*, an *Expert Jigsaw* and some critical reading strategies. But it can equally be used without this foundation, if appropriate, if a suitable topic or question is available.

Divide the class into small groups. Given that this exercise works best when there are around eight people on the panel, there should be eight groups in total. Ask them to spend fifteen minutes discussing the topic or the text. In doing so, encourage them to use anything readily at hand to research terms, gather data or explore different perspectives on the issue. Be clear with them that after fifteen minutes, they should have arrived at a standpoint, a group position on the topic at hand, and have built an evidence base from which to discuss the merits of their group position. In other words, the speakers on the panel will be arguing from an informed position, rather than an emotional or uninformed position.

At the conclusion, ask each small group to select one person who is to represent their views to the whole group – the speaker. Assemble the panel in a row, and arrange the other students in front of them.

The speakers' panel operates on a question and answer basis, where members of the class direct questions to a specific panel member, or to the whole panel. In so doing, strongly encourage them to ask level three questions (see pp. 119–120) which are analytical or evaluative and therefore are more likely to generate answers which will deepen the class's understanding of the topic. As the facilitator, it can be necessary to model the asking of rich questions, or to intervene if the panel is drifting away from the topic, again, with a pertinent question.

The speakers' panel should be run using the same discussion protocols as the *Socratic Seminar* (see p. 103) and *Philosophical Chairs* (see p. 123) – no side-chats, one person speaks at a time, each person listens carefully to what is said, everyone waits for three others to speak before they speak again. These protocols should be used by the panel and the rest of the class.

The decision about the duration of the speakers' panel can be made at any time. When it has served its purpose, close it down. For the most part, after thirty minutes, each panel member will have spoken at least once and twenty or more questions will have been asked and answered. As in the case of the *Socratic Seminar*, it is always better to leave a discussion when it is still alive, as it were, since this means that the participants will hopefully continue to discuss it after the end of the class.

Conclusion

The teaching strategies outlined here are clearly designed for students who have fairly significant gaps in their skill levels, for whom the habitus of a university might be understandably obscure or confusing. Laying bare the culture of the university through the explicit and transparent explanation of some of the protocols useful to pre-reading, working with text, critical analysis and developing oral fluency can make a significant difference to students' sense of belonging, self-confidence and, ultimately, their academic success (see Archer & Hutchings 2000; Devlin 2011; Gale & Mills 2013; Haggis 2006; Murphy 2009; Read *et al.* 2003; Richardson & Radloff 2014; Roberts 2011; Tangalakis *et al.* 2014; Tapp 2014).

Their use, however, should be judged carefully according to the student group and their relative familiarity with the practices and protocols required by universities. This raises the question of how best to proceed if the class is unevenly prepared for tertiary study – should one cater for the least or most prepared? Or somewhere in between? For the most part, the teaching strategies in this chapter are easily adapted to a wide variety of circumstances and since they are largely highly interactive, they are also highly engaging and diverse students can benefit from being exposed to them, both as a means of covering the class material but also as tools for developing critical academic skills.

Bibliography

Ahern, K.F. (2013) 'Tuning the sonic playing field: Teaching ways of knowing sound in first year writing', *Computers and Composition* 30(2): 75–86.

Amsler, S. (2014) '"By ones and twos and tens": Pedagogies of possibility for democratising higher education', *Pedagogy, Culture and Society* 22(2): 275–294.

Archer, L. (2007) 'Diversity, equality and higher education: A critical reflection on the ab/uses of equity discourse within widening participation', *Teaching in Higher Education* 12(5–6): 635–653.

Archer, L. & M. Hutchings (2000) '"Bettering yourself"? Discourses of risk, cost and benefit in ethnically diverse, young working-class non-participants' constructions of higher education', *British Journal of Sociology of Education* 21(4): 555–574.

Armstrong, D. & A. Cairnduff (2012) 'Inclusion in higher education: Issues in university–school partnership', *International Journal of Inclusive Education* 16(9): 917–928.

Aryadoust, V. (2015) 'Self- and peer assessments of oral presentations by first-year university students', *Educational Assessment* 20(3): 199–225.

Bachleitner, R. & M. Weichbold (2015) 'On the fundamental principles of visual sociology: Perceiving and seeing, observing and considering', *Forum Qualitative Sozialforschung* 16(2): 113–119.

Baleni, Z.G. (2015) 'Online formative assessment in higher education: Its pros and cons', *Electronic Journal of E-Learning* 13(4): 228–236.

Beall, J. (2015) 'Predatory journals and the breakdown of research cultures', *Information Development*, 31(5): 473–476.

Béres, I., T. Magyar & M. Turcsányi-Szabó (2012) 'Towards a personalised, learning style based collaborative blended learning model with individual assessment', *Informatics in Education* 11(1): 1–28.

Bhati, S.S. (2012) 'The effectiveness of oral presentation assessment in a finance subject: An empirical examination', *Journal of University Teaching & Learning Practice* 9(2): 1–21.

Bilić, P. (2015) '"Searching for a centre that holds" in the network society: Social construction of knowledge on, and with, English Wikipedia', *New Media & Society* 17(8): 1258–1276.

Bowser, D. & P.A. Danaher (2007) 'Indigenous, pre-undergraduate and international students at Central Queensland University, Australia: Three cases of the dynamic tension between diversity and commonality', *Teaching in Higher Education* 12(5–6): 669–681.

Bukowiecki, E., S. Miskelly, D. AuCoin, H. Burgiel, K. Evans, R. Farrar & S. Viveiros (2009) 'A center for academic achievement: How innovative collaborations between faculty and learning center administrators built model, credit-bearing, first-year courses with embedded support for at-risk students', *International Journal of Learning* 15(11): 65–77.

Carless, D. (2015) 'Exploring learning-oriented assessment processes', *Higher Education* 69(6): 963–976.

Carmichael, P. & M. MacMillan (2011) 'Teaching source credibility to undergraduates: A reflective dialogue', *Transformative Dialogues: Teaching and Learning Journal*, 4(3): 1–8.

Carolan, S. & C. Evain (2013). 'Self-publishing: Opportunities and threats in a new age of mass culture', *Publishing Research Quarterly* 29(4): 285–300.

Chamberlain, J.M., J. Hillier & P. Signoretta (2015) 'Counting better? An examination of the impact of quantitative method teaching on statistical anxiety and confidence', *Active Learning in Higher Education* 16(1): 51–66.

Charbonneau, D.H. (2015). 'Health disclaimers and website credibility markers', *Reference & User Services Quarterly*, 54(3): 30–36.

Christie, H., L. Tett, V.E. Cree, J. Hounsell & V. McCune (2008) '"A real rollercoaster of confidence and emotions": Learning to be a university student', *Studies in Higher Education* 33(5): 567–581.

Claydon, A. (2007) 'Analysing film through music', *International Journal of the Humanities* 4(7): 99–105.

Clegg, S., S. Bradley & K. Smith (2006) '"I've had to swallow my pride": Help seeking and self-esteem', *Higher Education Research and Development* 25(2): 101–113.

Collier, P.J. & D.L. Morgan (2008) '"Is that paper really due today?" Differences in first-generation and traditional college students' understandings of faculty expectations', *Higher Education* 55(4): 425–446.

Connelly, S., N.E. Dunbar, M.L. Jensen, J. Griffith, W.D. Taylor, G. Johnson & M.D. Mumford (2016) 'Social categorization, moral disengagement, and credibility of ideological group websites', *Journal of Media Psychology: Theories, Methods, and Applications* 28(1): 16–31.

Cooper, L. (2013). 'Trends in online academic publishing', *Metaphilosophy*, 44(3): 327–334.

Cortez, C., M. Nussbaum, G. Woywood & R. Aravena (2009) 'Learning to collaborate by collaborating: A face-to-face collaborative activity for measuring and learning basics about teamwork', *Journal of Computer Assisted Learning* 25(2): 126–142.

Costa, A. & B. Kallick (2008) *Learning and Leading with Habits of Mind*, Alexandria, VA: ASCD.

Dennis, J.M., J.S. Phinney & L.I. Chuateco (2005) 'The role of motivation, parental support, and peer support in the academic success of ethnic minority first-generation college students', *Journal of College Student Development* 46(3): 223–236.

Devlin, M. (2011) 'Bridging socio-cultural incongruity: Conceptualising the success of students from low socio-economic status backgrounds in Australian higher education', *Studies in Higher Education* 38(6): 939–949.

Dunbar, N.E., S. Connelly, M.L. Jensen, B.J. Adame, B. Rozzell, J.A. Griffith & H. Dan O'Hair (2014) 'Fear appeals, message processing cues, and credibility in the websites of violent, ideological, and nonideological groups', *Journal of Computer-Mediated Communication* 19(4): 871–889.

Edwards, S. & J. Bone (2012) 'Integrating peer assisted learning and eLearning: Using innovative pedagogies to support learning and teaching in higher education settings', *Australian Journal of Teacher Education* 37(5): 1–12.

Gale, T. & C. Mills (2013) 'Creating spaces in higher education for marginalised Australians: Principles for socially inclusive pedagogies', *Enhancing Learning in the Social Sciences* 5(2): 7–19.

García-Ros, R. (2011) 'Analysis and validation of a rubric to assess oral presentation skills in university contexts', *Electronic Journal of Research in Educational Psychology*, 9(3): 1043–1061.

Garz, M., A. Rott & M. Wass von Czege (2015) 'The online market for illegal copies of magazines: A German case study', *Journal of Broadcasting & Electronic Media*, 59(1): 169–183.

Go, E., K.H. You, E. Jung & H. Shim (2016). 'Why do we use different types of websites and assign them different levels of credibility? Structural relations among users' motives, types of websites, information credibility, and trust in the press', *Computers in Human Behavior* 5(4): 231–239.

Greenberg, S., E. Yaari & J. Bar-Ilan (2013) 'Perceived credibility of blogs on the internet – the influence of age on the extent of criticism', *Aslib Proceedings* 65(1): 4–18.

Guyver, R. (2012) 'Teaching historical thinking through contextualised sites, archives and artefacts', *Agora* 47(3): 52–57.

Haggis, T. (2006) 'Pedagogies for diversity: Retaining critical challenge amidst fears of "dumbing down"', *Studies in Higher Education* 31(5): 521–535.

Hall, G. (2013) 'The unbound book: Academic publishing in the age of the infinite archive', *Journal of Visual Culture* 12(3): 490–507.

Holbeck, R., S. Greenberger, L. Cooper, J. Steele, S.M. Palenque & S. Koukoudeas (2015) 'Reporting plagiarism in the online classroom', *Journal of Online Learning & Teaching* 11(2): 202–209.

Holmes, N.G., C.E. Wieman & D.A. Bonn (2015) 'Teaching critical thinking', *Proceedings of the National Academy of Sciences of the United States of America* 112(36): 11199–11204.

Ison, D.C. (2014) 'Does the online environment promote plagiarism? A comparative study of dissertations from brick-and-mortar versus online institutions', *Journal of Online Learning & Teaching* 10(2): 272–281.

James, D. (2014) 'Investigating the curriculum through assessment practice in higher education: The value of a "learning cultures" approach', *Higher Education* 67(2): 155–169.

Johnson-Glenberg, M.C. (2010) 'Embedded formative e-assessment: Who benefits, who falters', *Educational Media International* 47(2): 153–171.

Krathwohl, D.R. (2002) 'A revision of Bloom's taxonomy: An overview', *Theory into Practice* 41(4): 212–218.

Leidenfrost, B., B. Strassnig, M. Schütz, C. Carbon & A. Schabmann (2014) 'The impact of peer mentoring on mentee academic performance: Is any mentoring style better than no mentoring at all?', *International Journal of Teaching & Learning in Higher Education* 26(1): 102–111.

Leitch, T.M. (2014) *Wikipedia U: Knowledge, Authority and Liberal Education in the Digital Age*, Baltimore, MD: Johns Hopkins University Press.

Leon, J.S., K. Winskell, D.A. McFarland & C. del Rio (2015) 'A case-based, problem-based learning approach to prepare master of public health candidates for the complexities of global health', *American Journal of Public Health* 105(4): S92–S96.

Losh, E. (2014) *The War on Learning. Gaining Ground in the Digital University*, Boston, MA: MIT Press.

McCabe, M.J. & C.M. Snyder (2014). 'Identifying the effect of open access on citations using a panel of science journals', *Economic Inquiry* 52(4): 1284–1300.

McCarthy, J. (2015) 'Evaluating written, audio and video feedback in higher education summative assessment tasks', *Issues in Educational Research* 25(2): 153–169.

MacMillan, M. (2014) 'Student connections with academic texts: A phenomenographic study of reading', *Teaching in Higher Education* 19(8): 943–954.

Moeed, A. (2015) 'Theorizing formative assessment: Time for a change in thinking', *Educational Forum* 79(2): 180–189.

Monge, R. & E. Frisicaro-Pawlowski (2014) 'Redefining information literacy to prepare students for the 21st century workforce', *Innovative Higher Education* 39(1): 59–73.

Morrison, A. (2010) '"I want an education": Two cases of working class ambition and ambivalence in further and higher education', *Research in Post-Compulsory Education* 15(1): 175–185.

Murphy, B. (2009) 'Great expectations? Progression and achievement of less traditional entrants to higher education', *Widening Participation and Lifelong Learning* 11(2): 4–14.

Murphy, K. & S. Barry (2016) 'Feed-forward: Students gaining more from assessment via deeper engagement in video-recorded presentations', *Assessment and Evaluation in Higher Education* 41(2): 213–227.

O'Sullivan, D. (2009) *Wikipedia: A New Community of Practice?*, Farnham, UK: Ashgate.

Özkan, G. & G.S. Selçuk (2013) 'The use of conceptual change texts as class material in the teaching of "sound" in physics', *Asia-Pacific Forum on Science Learning & Teaching* 14(1): 1–22.

Pacello, J. (2014) 'Integrating metacognition into a developmental reading and writing course to promote skill transfer: An examination of student perceptions and experiences', *Journal of College Reading & Learning* 44(2): 119–140.

Peach, D. (2005) 'Ensuring student success: The role of support services in improving the quality of the student learning experience', *Studies in Learning, Evaluation, Innovation and Development* 2(3): 1–15.

Pearce, J., B. Down & E. Moore (2008) 'Social class, identity and the "good" student: Negotiating university culture', *Australian Journal of Education* 52(3): 257–271.

Radford, L. (2014) 'On the role of representations and artefacts in knowing and learning', *Educational Studies in Mathematics* 85(3): 405–422.

Rahim, P.A. (2013) 'Pedagogy for meeting the challenges of tackling reading amongst university students', *Procedia – Social and Behavioral Sciences, 107 (The Proceedings of the 1st Evaluation of Learning for Performance Improvement International Conference 2013)*: 72–79.

Read, B., L. Archer & C. Leathwood (2003) 'Challenging cultures? Student conceptions of "belonging" and "isolation" at a post-1992 university', *Studies in Higher Education* 28(3): 261–277.

Read, J. & J. Von Randow (2013) 'A university post-entry English language assessment: Charting the changes', *International Journal of English Studies* 13(2): 89–110.

Richardson, S. & A. Radloff (2014) 'Allies in learning: Critical insights into the importance of staff–student interactions in university education', *Teaching in Higher Education* 19(6): 603–615.

Roberts, S. (2011) 'Traditional practice for non-traditional students? Examining the role of pedagogy in higher education retention', *Journal of Further and Higher Education* 35(2): 183–199.

Rush, S.C. (2014) 'Transana qualitative video and audio analysis software as a tool for teaching intellectual assessment skills to graduate psychology students', *Journal of Educational Technology Systems* 43(1): 55–74.

Ryan, M. & D. Brough (2012) 'Reflections around artefacts: Using a deliberative approach to teaching reflective practices in fashion studies', *Journal of Learning Design* 5(1): 1–11.

Schroeder, R. & L. Taylor (2015) 'Big data and Wikipedia research: Social science knowledge across disciplinary divides', *Information, Communication & Society* 18(9): 1039–1056.

Singh, G. & G. Hardaker (2014) 'Barriers and enablers to adoption and diffusion of eLearning: A systematic review of the literature – a need for an integrative approach', *Education + Training* 56(2–3): 105–121.

Subramaniam, M., N. Taylor, B. St Jean, R. Follman, C. Kodama & D. Casciotti (2015) 'As simple as that?: Tween credibility assessment in a complex online world', *Journal of Documentation* 71(3): 550–571.

Tahiroğlu, K., O. Özcan & A. Ikonen (2014) 'Sound in new media and design studies', *Design Issues* 30(2): 56–66.

Tangalakis, K., K. Hughes, C. Brown & K. Dickson (2014) 'The use of explicit teaching strategies for academic staff and students in science foundation subjects', *International Journal of Innovation in Science and Mathematics Education* 22(3): 42–51.

Tapp, J. (2014) '"I actually listened, I'm proud of myself": The effects of a participatory pedagogy on students' constructions of academic identities', *Teaching in Higher Education* 19(4): 323–335.

Tariq, V.N. & N. Durrani (2012) 'Factors influencing undergraduates' self-evaluation of numerical competence', *International Journal of Mathematical Education in Science and Technology* 43(3): 337–356.

Tariq, V.N., P. Qualter, S. Roberts, Y. Appleby & L. Barnes (2013) 'Mathematical literacy in undergraduates: Role of gender, emotional intelligence and emotional self-efficacy', *International Journal of Mathematical Education in Science and Technology* 44(8): 1143–1159.

Torenbeek, M., E. Jansen & W. Hofman (2011). 'Predicting first-year achievement by pedagogy and skill development in the first weeks at university', *Teaching in Higher Education* 16(6): 655–668.

Turner, K., L. Roberts, C. Heal & L. Wright (2013) 'Oral presentation as a form of summative assessment in a master's level PGCE module: The student perspective', *Assessment & Evaluation in Higher Education* 38(6): 662–673.

Valanto, V., M. Kosonen & H. Ellonen, (2015) 'Are publishers ready for tomorrow? Publishers' capabilities and online innovations', *International Journal of Innovation Management* 16 (1): 1250001–1250001–1250001–1250018.

van Ginkel, S., J. Gulikers, H. Biemans & M. Mulder (2015) 'Review: Towards a set of design principles for developing oral presentation competence: A synthesis of research in higher education', *Educational Research Review* 14: 62–80.

van Rooij, S.W. & K. Zirkle (2016) 'Balancing pedagogy, student readiness and accessibility: A case study in collaborative online course development', *The Internet and Higher Education* 28: 1–7.

Wilkinson, T., M. Boohan & M. Stevenson (2014) 'Does learning style influence academic performance in different forms of assessment?', *Journal of Anatomy* 224(3): 304–308.

Chapter 5

Collaboration

Introduction

Sometimes called 'cooperative learning' (Johnson & Johnson 2009), 'active learning' (Braxton *et al.* 2000; Braxton *et al.* 2008) or 'participatory pedagogy' (Tapp 2014), collaborative learning practices – when compared with individualistic and competitive practices – are an extremely effective way of generating student engagement, increasing student success and ultimately supporting persistence rather than attrition. A meta-analysis of 1,200 studies conducted in universities and other adult settings over the last 110 years, for example, showed that classroom collaboration results in higher achievement, greater productivity, improved relationships, improved psychological health, self-esteem and social competence (Johnson & Johnson 2009). Whilst there are a number of causes of this effect, foremost amongst them appear to be activity (or rather a lack of passivity) and the students' sense that they are known and valued (Michaelsen *et al.* 2002; Persell *et al.* 2008). The teaching strategies described in chapter 3 are all designed to establish a culture of affinity, warmth and a sense of belonging which lay the foundation for further work on building an active and engaged classroom with all the benefits which flow from this – for both the students and the teacher.

Aside from the general, warm culture which Allen (2008), amongst others, argues is so important are three further factors which both enrich teaching, and produce an ongoing positive effect on student outcomes: the explicit approval of students' classroom contributions; interest in, and enthusiasm for, the students' work; and numerous teacher/student interactions in the classroom (Hourigan 2013; Read *et al.* 2003; Richardson & Radloff 2014; Roberts 2011; Tapp 2014).

These qualities should be actively and purposefully articulated and promoted to be effective. When they are, Hourigan (2013) contends, student engagement and cooperation rise as does their motivation level. De Hei *et al.* (2015) go further to argue that the literature on collaborative learning clearly shows that it doesn't only have an effect on emotional and pro-social development, but importantly also on cognition. Crucially, the foundation for collaboration, as outlined above, must be established in order for it to work well for both the students and the teaching staff who use it. Without such a foundation, De Hei *et al.* found four common outcomes in student group work: disputes between students; variance in commitment to the group and the task (typically when one or more participant(s) becomes a 'passenger'); poor communication between the students and the teacher over the division of tasks; and a lack of acceptance (or rejection) of feedback from other group members, and a preoccupation with feedback from the teacher.

A relatively simple way to pre-empt such difficulties is to (again) be explicit with the group about these possible difficulties and to discuss the ways in which they are to be dealt with. The precursor of such a discussion is to establish the following:

1. How the groups are to be formed (homogeneous or heterogeneous? voluntary or forced?)
2. Role clarity – who is going to do what?
3. Scheduling meetings – how frequently and where? It is wise to promote consideration of family responsibilities, location, work commitments, any student physical limitations or constraints
4. How will a lack of commitment or work be dealt with by the group? How might it be reflected in the group's mark?

Such a discussion reflects the *Social Contract* discussed in chapter 3, and uses a similar method for establishing its principles. Students, therefore, should be familiar with the protocols of making such an agreement, and equally familiar with the commitment which making such an arrangement entails.

There is a strong argument for the use of collaborative learning not simply because it increases student engagement and therefore retention – but because the ability to work effectively in a team is an almost ubiquitous 'graduate attribute' in contemporary universities (Braxton *et al.* 2000; Braxton *et al.* 2008; Davidson *et al.* 2014; Michaelsen *et al.* 2002; Thompson *et al.* 2012). This skill can be scaffolded and articulated as being critical to their developing expertise as professionals in their field – it enables them to practise and improve their ability to cooperate with others, solve problems and work to deadlines.

The following teaching strategies are designed to purposefully develop the ability of students to cooperate for mutual benefit. They can be wrapped around any teaching material in any discipline (see for examples Gaunt & Westerlund 2013; Hourigan 2013; Johnson & Johnson 2009; Lanqin *et al.* 2015; Popov *et al.* 2014; Tangalakis *et al.* 2014; Tekbiyik 2015; Thompson *et al.* 2012). Again, it is critical to articulate their purpose and their efficacy to students as you go through them – explain why you are using them and how they will enable students to build their skills in a safe environment, for use when they are working on assessed group projects and later, for professional teamwork in the workplace.

I Discussion Protocols

This is a fast, collaborative exercise which complements the *Social Contract* (see p. 53) and the rules of engagement for a *Socratic Seminar* (see p. 103) and works as a general precursor to the following teaching strategies which rely, for their success, on relatively orderly discussions. A judgement can be made about whether or not the group needs this confirmation of collaborative classroom protocols and it can often be omitted. However, if there is doubt about the level at which the class is collaborating, or a sense that another step is needed, this strategy can be helpful. If it is to be used, this is best done the week prior to the first *Socratic Seminar*.

Firstly, split the class into small groups of three to five people – either homogeneous or heterogeneous (i.e. with friends or with those they don't often collaborate with). Ask each group to draw up three standards they believe are essential for successful and collaborative classroom discussions. Provide approximately ten minutes for this, shortening the time if there is any evidence of disengagement or side-chats.

Secondly, ask each group to display their standards. This can be done on the whiteboard, or using any visible aids to hand. Equally, it can be done quickly by asking them to read them out, whilst the teachers writes them on the whiteboard or something similar. As each group participates, blend any two which appear similar in order to avoid repetition.

When this stage is complete, the class votes for the five most important protocols – most commonly by a show of hands. Again, this can be done simply by counting and recording the numbers of votes next to each protocol on the board.

The final stage is the establishment of the most voted-for protocols as the basic principles for discussion for that group.

The benefit of using this stepped-out exercise is that it provides clarity of expectation, it involves the whole group making the decisions around protocols (rather than just the teacher), and this in turn creates a sense of ownership of the protocols and the resultant likelihood that they will be adhered to. In addition, it promotes the sense that the classroom is an inclusive, safe environment which enables students to take risks.

2 Think-Pair-Share

Another strategy which develops collaboration, this strategy is commonly used in secondary education, but is equally applicable to tertiary settings. Taking approximately twenty minutes to complete, it has the advantage of enabling students to create their individual response to a question, test their ideas on someone else, explore the similarities and differences between their response and that of their partner and then to co-create a joint response. This process involves a range of collaborative, critical thinking and negotiation skills whilst offering a safe platform through which to express ideas.

Firstly, provide the class with a question related to the week's topic, and share the activity's rationale and process. In order to be generative, this is best a dichotomous, controversial, Level Three question (see pp. 119–120).

Provide five to ten minutes for each person to consider the question and to write a one-page response to it, including their rationale and evidence for writing such a response.

Then ask them to find a partner. This can equally be achieved by the partnerships being formed purposefully by the teacher, or by requesting that they work with someone new.

Each partnership sits together and one person reads their response, whilst the other simply listens. Then the roles are reversed. Timing these exchanges increases engagement by ensuring that they are under a little pressure – around two minutes each works well.

At the conclusion, they are provided with five to seven minutes to build a jointly agreed response to the question through working collaboratively across points of agreement and disagreement (if any). In so doing, they should provide the evidence for their claims, and make an assessment of the credibility of that evidence. Again, be explicit with them about the time allowance for this.

If time allows, and it seems appropriate, this stage can be repeated by each pair joining another and the resulting groups of four producing a collective response. This reduces the time spent on the final stage (given that there are half the number of groups).

The final stage involves some or all of the pairs or groups volunteering to share their response with the class. There should be sufficient trust for this to be easy, but if it is not, debrief the causes of any unease with the group, again being open and transparent about the goals of collaboration, and why they are so important.

3 Zap the Problem

This is a widely used technique across numbers of professions and discipline areas that is useful for simple problem solving, but like the other collaborative techniques, it also uses the resources of the students and provides them with a sense of providing for the common good (Lovejoy 1988). Fundamentally an individualistic problem-solving exercise, it also builds cooperation and trust.

Zap the Problem takes around fifteen minutes to complete, but is relatively fast-paced.

Form groups of six or so students, ideally positioned around a table. Again, these groups can be formed purposefully or not, according to the teaching context.

Ask each class member to write a question they have about the topic of the week, or the material the class has covered that day, at the top of an A4 piece of paper. Emphasise the need for a question, not a statement. Emphasise that the question should be of use to them, and that every question should, and will, be respected by the participants. If a safe, cooperative culture has been built in the classroom through the use of the community-building strategies set out in chapter 3, it is unlikely that there will be any judgement made about the questions, but if there is, it is crucial to be explicit about the purpose of the activity (to clear up any misunderstandings). This is a private exercise, with no general feedback loop, and this should help to facilitate students' sense of safety in the questions which they share.

Provide them with three minutes to consider and write their question. It is productive to encourage them to use Level Three questions for this (see pp. 119–120), rather than Level One or Two questions since these are relatively easy to answer without the students engaging any higher-level thinking skills.

After three minutes, ask that each person pass their A4 sheet with their question, to the person on their right. They will then collect their neighbour's question from their left. They then write an answer to the question they have received.

It is important to time this, giving them two minutes to complete, since this develops a stronger sense of engagement and urgency. If you have requested that they use Level Three questions, it will be unlikely that they are unable to answer the question they encounter, but you might consider offering the possibility to 'pass' if they are stuck. If you decide to allow them to do this, it may well mean that participants don't fully engage with the activity – but this is a matter of judgement.

Rotate the papers around the table until each person has a set of answers to their question. With groups of six, this will take around twelve minutes to complete but by the conclusion, each individual will have six answers to their question. This technique need not be situated within course material; you can equally enable them to ask more generalised questions about any difficulty they are having with their study, or life on campus.

Zap the Problem can be extremely useful as a closing exercise for a topic, a class or even a teaching session. It can also be used as a method of revision, prior to summative assessment. It draws on the expertise in the room, and offers students a private method of gaining answers to their questions.

4 Team Building

Similar in tone to the Stage One group builder called *Weird Connections*, this exercise is designed both to find affinities between class members, and to team build. It is particularly useful as a precursor to undertaking group assignments, which can be challenging, particularly when there are varying levels of commitment and ability amongst the group.

Depending on whether the group has been purposefully built to ensure a range of competencies, or the students have selected themselves, this exercise can build a much higher level of commitment. It requires coloured pens and paper for each group. It should take around fifteen minutes to complete, but can be economical in terms of later saving the time spent on resolving disputes and difficulties arising from problematic groups.

1 Ask each group to sit together.
2 Each group is then to choose a name for their team. What do they have in common? What are their differences? What do they agree on? If it seems appropriate, at this stage you can ask them to build a mini-social contract (see the *Social Contract* in chapter 3) in order that their expectations are explicitly laid out and shared.

3 With the people at their table, they then create a visual symbol for their team, with the name, and place it on their table. Allow approximately seven minutes for this.
4 Ask each team to share these images and the team's reasoning with the whole class, asking for a spokesperson from each team to do this.

This activity can help students to bond early on – particularly if they are going to have to work closely together. It has the additional advantage of laying the foundations for productive group work in that the participants' skill sets will be displayed through the symbolic illustration, through the thought-leadership when devising a name and through the person selected to present to the whole class.

If it seems as if particular personalities are dominating (which sometimes happens), a diverting addition can be made to the fourth stage of this process. Called 'The Flying Fickle Finger of Fate', you can ask each group to point their finger at the person best placed to present to the group. When there is a dominant character present, almost invariably they will be chosen by the majority. At this point, you ask that person chosen to choose someone else to present. Lead this by focussing the whole group's attention on each table at a time.[1]

5 Jigsaw

Created in the 1970s, this teaching strategy has been used very successfully for forty years in both schools and universities (Aronson and Patnoe 2011). It was originally designed to facilitate and generate friendships across different demographic groups in classrooms. As its name suggests, it is based on the notion that each member of a group makes a contribution to a final 'picture', or understanding, which can only be completed with each person's contribution. As such, it requires the equal contribution of each member of the group.

There are two versions of this activity – a simple jigsaw and an expert jigsaw – both described next.

In a tertiary setting, jigsaws can be an extremely time-efficient, collaborative means of breaking a large task down. One example is its use to help students tackle a complex reading task. Other methods of doing this are also available in the following chapter.

Break the class into small groups (either purposeful or accidental) and divide the reading into sections. A page per person is ideal. You can allocate more than this if it seems appropriate and also provide it in the previous week so that they arrive with the reading already done. If any member hasn't completed their section for any reason, this can be difficult, although if you have successfully built a dialogic, cooperative classroom culture, there will automatically be a strong incentive to have completed their section of the reading since failing to do so would mean disappointing other group members.

Whether they will read on the spot, or have already completed the reading, each person's responsibility is to provide the other group members with an account of their section of the reading. Start with the first section and follow consecutively. This should take in the region of twenty minutes – depending of course on the length of the piece. As they undertake this, move through the room checking for understanding levels and for the level of their engagement and participation.

To conclude, ask for feedback. What did the first part say? The second? And so forth. You can use this time to clear up any misunderstandings, and to clarify any terms or vocabulary which they have struggled with.

At the end, all students should have a robust working knowledge of the reading which has been achieved relatively quickly, and which is now available for further activities.

6 Expert Jigsaw

A slightly more complex version of a jigsaw, the *Expert Jigsaw* has an additional effect – it facilitates the bonding of each participant with two groups – their 'home' group, and their 'expert' group. Again, it is dependent on the notion that each involved person contributes one piece of a task, and that with every piece in place, each group and the whole class will come to an understanding of something within a tight timeframe, yet drawing on the expertise of the whole group.

As in a simple jigsaw, divide the reading or task into sections and allocate a section to each participant. You can do this by simply numbering 1–5, for example, which will produce fairly heterogeneous groups and move individuals away from friends or people they've worked with before. As such, this is useful when classes have developed subgroups, or even subcultures, since it forces people to interact closely with those they may not know well.

Each small group will become expert on their section of the text or task. Rearrange them in order that they are all sitting together – section 1 at one table, section 2 at another, and so on. Ask those looking at the first section to become experts on it, and do the same for the following parts. They do this through an exchange of ideas, an analysis of their piece. The process should be given around ten minutes, and at the conclusion, the small group should have an agreed-upon position on its content, purpose, argument and so forth. Encourage them to take short notes which summarise what the group has said, since these notes can act as an *aide-memoire*, and provide a foundation for their contribution to their home group.

When that is complete, they return to their 'home' group, and each participant acts as an expert on their part of the text or task. They recount the experts' position on that section. When each participant has provided this, the group should have a comprehensive understanding of the reading or task at hand. Again, this activity depends on equal participation by every person – in both the groups they are responsible to.

Like the simple jigsaw, this is a highly collaborative activity which has the benefit of positioning students as experts on a small part of a large task, which can be very supportive, developing their sense of themselves as scholars. In addition, it offers a scaffolded approach where they can test their ideas with others, develop a position, then offer this position to their 'home' group as an expert. This lays the basis for the Critical Thinking teaching strategies laid out in chapter 6.

Finally, like the other strategies, this activity can be concluded by building a whole-group picture of the article or other resource. This can be achieved by asking each group to report on the whole thing, or reporting section by section. In either case, as they report, use visuals to assist either as a list on the whiteboard, a diagram or an infographic – whatever seems to be the most helpful to the class and to your material.

7 ACAPS (Author, Context, Audience, Purpose, Significance)

This strategy uses the same scheme as the *Expert Jigsaw* insofar as small groups of five are formed, either strategically or not, with each group assigned to examining a specific part of a text, image, artefact, sound recording, graph, table, website, infographic, blog, wiki or anything else which seems appropriate for your purposes.

This is an extremely effective and successful strategy which works well across disciplinary boundaries, and across a wide range of resources (adapted from Custer *et al.* 2011). It can be a particularly useful starting point for a topic given that it enables students to explore what they know already – or can guess – about the thing you share with them. It has been successfully employed with audio recordings (of speeches, for example), images (of news events, for example), artefacts (such as letters, ornaments, clothing, objects, for example), media opinion pieces, websites or anything else which is of interest to your topic, and which will stimulate discussion and interest. A historical photograph works as well as the periodic table for this exercise.

As in the *Expert Jigsaw* above, number the class 1–5 and give each a task (author, context, audience, purpose or significance). Ask all the number ones (audience) to sit together, the numbers twos (context) to sit together and so on through to five.

Each group is responsible for coming to a standpoint on their particular aspect of the topic. The resources which you allow them to use for this can be varied according to the situation. If, for example, you permit them to use the Internet to fully research the matter under consideration, this reduces the benefit of this collaborative exercise facilitating a simple question and answer scenario. An example of this would be if they were provided with a photograph of a historical moment – they can very simply find the name of the event, the photographer, where it first appeared and so forth. On balance, the teaching strategy becomes more powerful if each group depends on their own resources and prior knowledge, and through enquiry, all come to a combined position on their part of the exercise.

Ask each group to consider the following:

1 Author – Who created the object under consideration? What do you know about this person and their point of view? Does this point of view create the source's meaning?

2   Context – In what social context was the object created? When was it created? Where was it created? Does this change the way in which the object should be considered?
3   Audience – Whom was it created for? Does knowledge of the intended audience change the object's meaning?
4   Purpose – Why was this object created? How might this affect its meaning?
5   Significance – What can be drawn or inferred from this object? What is its main idea? Why is it important?

You should allow around fifteen minutes for this discussion.

When complete, ask them to return to their 'home' table, as in the *Expert Jigsaw* above, and to share their findings with the rest of the group. Allow around twenty minutes for this, followed by a whole-class dialogue of their findings and the discussion which led them to their findings. At the end of this process, there should be a comprehensive understanding of the object under consideration, and an appreciation of the combined input which generated their understanding.

ACAPS helps students' sense of self-confidence as they reveal and combine what they already know, and can be particularly useful before beginning a new topic. This is useful for opening up discussion and empowering students by showing them that they already have background knowledge on the topic. It also helps them to learn collaboratively, building trust levels and relationships in much the same way as jigsaws were designed to do (Aronson & Patnoe 2011). Like the *Socratic Seminar* below, this exercise is rich enough to form the focal point of a one-hour class, allowing a whole-group consideration of an object, or source, of merit.

8 Socratic Seminars

When done well, *Socratic Seminars* are a powerful tool to generate collaborative learning. They develop students' questioning skills, their discussion skills, their research skills and they can improve their critical thinking within a structured framework. Unlike the collaborative strategies covered so far, *Socratic Seminars* have relatively formal protocols which it is important to follow with care if the seminar is to be successful. As such, they have been used in a variety of teaching contexts and they are, of course, based on Socrates' notion of teaching using developing questions (see Chowning 2009; Davies & Sinclair 2014; Kingsley 2011; Mitchell 2006; Tredway 1995). Used in secondary education for many years to teach adolescents the skills of conducting a considered, inquiry-based discussion (Roberts & Billings 1999), *Socratic Seminars* are no less powerful for tertiary students who may struggle with engaging in formal conversations, and who welcome explicit behaviour protocols to guide them in their thinking and discussion.

For any successful *Socratic Seminar* there are four equally important elements that need to be in place:

1. **An object** which is to be explored in the seminar. Typically, this is text but depending on the discipline, it can be anything which is both interesting and pertinent to the week's topic. Images, artefacts, music, speeches, graphs or tables are all equally useful.
2. **A key question** which the seminar is to address. This should be an open-ended, Level Three question which participants are likely to find thought-provoking. A good question should elicit interest from the students, and strongly connect them to the object under consideration. It is advisable to choose a question which is itself provocative since this will prompt students to form and express opinions.
3. **The facilitator**, whose role it is to ensure that the protocols (see below) are followed closely. Quite formal by intention, without these protocols the seminar can dissipate into a messy discussion, but with them can be a great learning tool. The facilitator ensures that the seminar keeps on task (on the object, answering the key question), asking questions which deepen the discussion or which boost the discussion. Importantly, they also ensure that quieter members of the class are provided with the time to participate, and that more dominating students are explicitly constrained.
4. **The participants** are also responsible for ensuring that the seminar is orderly, that it stays on topic and that the protocols are followed. In part, they do this by learning to listen carefully to what their classmates say, ensuring that they add to the discussion, share ideas, look for evidence for claims and work collaboratively. This simple process also helps the development of habits of mind which assist students to do well in their studies more generally – particularly if you debrief after the seminar, reflecting on what went well, how it can be improved next time and so forth. As a general rule, students become more comfortable – and more disciplined – in the way they have *Socratic Seminars* after their first two. Equally, facilitators become more skilled at learning and understanding what works best (adapted from Custer *et al.* 2011).

The participants, of course, should be quite clear about the expectations attached to this exercise in order that they are able to understand the reasons for undertaking it, and that they understand the rules of engagement which are, in short:

- That each person listens to what each participant says
- That each speaker paraphrases their colleague's prior contribution before they begin their own
- That they keep on topic
- That there are no side-chats or interruptions of the speaker

- That they agree to work with the others to deepen and widen the group's understanding of the topic.

In practice, it is common to have participants direct their comments and eye contact towards the facilitator, and for this reason, it is sensible for the facilitator to stand to one side, actively avoiding eye contact, but intervening if the discussion goes off-topic, if any participant tries to dominate the seminar or if any participants are not participating. If this occurs, you can use a token system whereby each person is given three per seminar and, as they speak, they 'spend' one of their tokens by placing it in a container. Similarly, the facilitator can use a 1–2–3–me protocol in a context where there are dominant personalities. This involves each person agreeing that they can only speak after three others have spoken. Although these might appear to be stringent procedures, they are very effective at subverting any situation lacking in collegiality, or where two inexperienced participants attempt to establish a one-on-one argument. If this occurs – as it commonly does – it is critical that the facilitator intervenes and in so doing is clear about the cause of their intervention. At the conclusion of the *Socratic Seminar*, it is very helpful for the whole group to reflect on its success, and the ways in which it might be improved next time. This facilitates self-reflection on the part of the participants, a skill particularly useful for other exercises using group work.

Before the seminar, whether it takes the simple or the more complex formation, make sure that the participants are clear about the rules of engagement:

- Use the key question as the starting point of the seminar.
- Refer to the object which the seminar is exploring or discussing.
- Make sure you have evidence for any claims you make – personal experiences and anecdotes are not helpful.
- Take turns speaking, making sure that at least three people have spoken before you speak again.
- Speak clearly.
- Don't engage in side conversations.
- Stay on topic.
- Listen carefully and respectfully to the points being made.
- Paraphrase the contribution of the previous speaker prior to making your own point.
- Reflect on the key question at the conclusion. Was it answered? How well?

Simple Socratic Seminar

This should be used with groups of ten or fewer. If the class is much larger than this, it is possible to have one, two or three seminars running simultaneously in a classroom, although this is not ideal because the facilitator could be spread very thinly. In this model, arrange the chairs in a formal, evenly spaced circle where

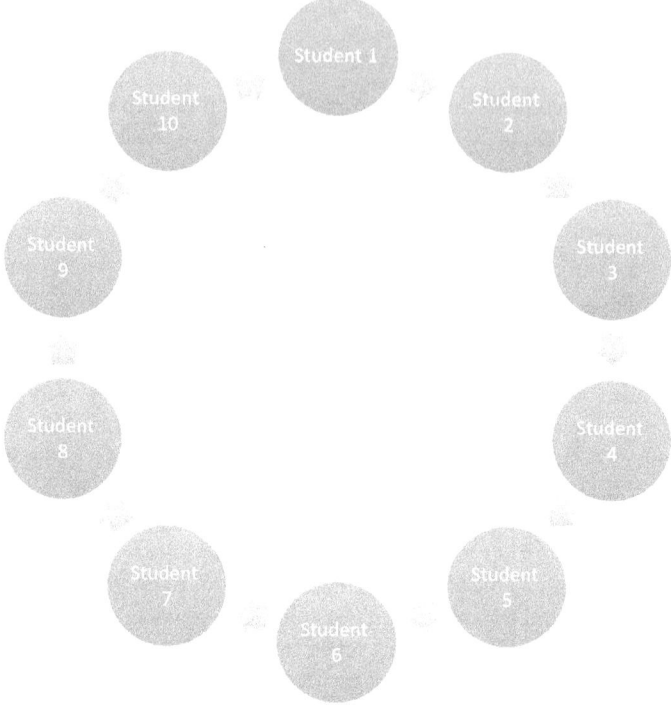

Figure 5.1 Simple *Socratic Seminar*

participants can see one another easily without leaning forwards or backwards (see Figure 5.1).

Complex Socratic Seminar

This model can be used with larger groups. It uses the same basic formation of a circle of ten people as above, but this is enriched by giving each speaker one or two Research Assistants, depending on the numbers in the group. In other words, if you have twenty people, each person in the circle has one Research Assistant; if you have thirty, each person has two Research Assistants. But one can adjust these numbers to suit the context.

Again, the students sit in a formal, easily accessible circle. The RAs sit behind them (see Figure 5.2).

Give each triad ten minutes to prepare their thoughts on the key question before the seminar begins. Encourage them to have a generalised discussion of their agreed-upon standpoint so far. This enables them to explore what they think, and practise what they will argue in the seminar.

During the seminar, the RAs' job is to help the person develop their argument by giving them input (suggestions, data). They can use the Internet or any other

Collaboration 105

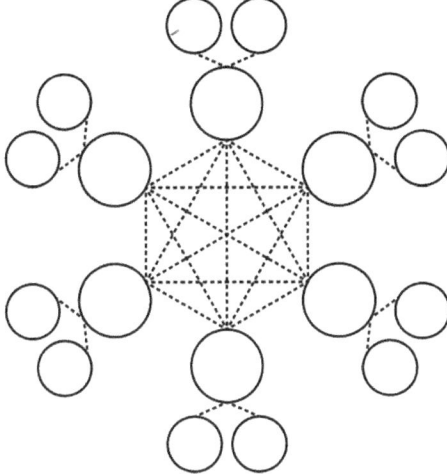

Figure 5.2 Socratic Seminar with Research Assistants

resource to do research and feed it into the discussion. Suggest that they use notes to pass their suggestions or comments to the person in the inner circle. They are not, at this stage, permitted to speak, since if they do, attention is drawn away from the central discussion circle and it can very quickly become dissipated and chaotic.

The RAs and the speaker in the triad are rotated in order that everyone has the opportunity to make their contribution. On the whole, a fifteen-minute rotation is an excellent model, occupying forty-five minutes of class time with ten minutes for preparation. As with all teaching strategies, this is flexible, so time can be spent as appropriate in each situation.

Perhaps unsurprisingly, this more complex and active formation can generate a lot of bustle and without a very active facilitator, can become fractured. It is crucial, therefore, to ensure that the students are explicitly reminded of the *Socratic Seminar* protocols if they are broken. These are best displayed in the room or, alternatively, provided to each individual participant.

Concluding a seminar is best done at the point where discussion is waning, but not yet concluded, however long that takes. If the seminar ends whilst the participants are still engaged in the topic, their questioning and interest continue.

Commonly, students initially find *Socratic Seminars* awkward and uncomfortable – partly because the seminar is so carefully constructed and doesn't allow for natural conversation. Be open about this, and explicit about the way in which participants adjust to the protocols used in *Socratic Seminars*. Both the participants and facilitators typically become more practised at conducting *Socratic Seminars* after the first one or two.

They are a highly effective strategy for developing students' formal discussion skills, listening skills, speaking skills and critical thinking skills.

9 Position Line

Socratic Seminars can be enhanced by inviting the participants to take a stand on the question under interrogation in the seminar – both before and after. This can be done in two simple ways:

1. By asking the class to stand in a dichotomous line with 'agree' at one end and 'disagree' at the other. At the conclusion, ask them to repeat this line, noting whether they have moved or not. If they moved along the position line, ask them to explain why they moved. In particular, ask them to pinpoint the moment when they decided to change their position. One possible disadvantage for this method is that it lacks privacy. If a contentious issue is under discussion, participants might feel exposed.
2. By drawing a line on the whiteboard, or placing a sticky note with 'agree' at one end of a wall and a note with 'disagree' at the other. Participants then place a sticky note (with their name or a symbol) somewhere along that continuum at the start and conclusion of the seminar. Afterwards, the group can evaluate the position changes made, and the arguments which led to those changes. Participants can volunteer their reasoning for changing their position along the continuum.

This quick exercise can be a valuable addition to a *Socratic Seminar* since it forces students to form an opinion, take a stand, then revise that opinion based on the seminar discussion. In so doing, it indicates that the discussion is serious and meaningful and that it is advantageous to pay close attention to the discussion.

10 The World Café

The creator of this teaching strategy argued that its purpose was 'making collective knowledge visible' (Brown 2002: 4). It also provides students with the opportunity to work collaboratively and systematically through a complex problem. Whilst *Socratic Seminars* and *Philosophical Chairs*, for example, are founded on the basis of dichotomous statements, and participants are encouraged to take a stand, to revise that stand and then to take a new stand after their consideration of the arguments and data put to them, the *World Café* is founded on the consideration of a staged, complex problem. But it can also be very effectively employed as a method of revising material. Farr (2013), for example, offers a useful case study of its use in this context, arguing that it was extremely successful in terms of the students' success rates. It is also perhaps the most multifaceted teaching strategy under discussion here since it involves a wide range of skills developed in the earlier techniques – formal discussion, collaboration, cooperation, critical thinking and inquiry (Brown & Isaacs 2005; Goodin & Stein 2008).

It gives students the opportunity to work through a complex problem in a collaborative way which enables them to build on the understanding of their peers. It also uses collaborative group work to investigate an issue or a problem, inviting them to view that issue or problem from multiple angles.

If the *World Café* is to be used, ensure that there is at least an hour to complete it – this is a strategy which can take some time, but is worth it. You will also need large pieces of flip chart paper, some coloured pens and a classroom where there is sufficient room for three large tables which will act as 'stations', and enough space for the participants to move freely between these tables. In addition, a case study, problem or narrative should be made available with a three-staged series of questions. Each participant should be provided with a copy of this case study, problem or narrative. Of course, it is advantageous to build the issue to be explored in such a way as to make good use of the students' prior knowledge of the course material, and to extend that knowledge. An example follows below.

Firstly, divide your participants into groups of three to five – depending on your numbers. Give each group part one of your case study, problem or narrative. Ask them to read it, look over the questions, discuss them in their small groups and to write their responses to the questions, and their key ideas, on their flip chart paper. In all, this should take ten to fifteen minutes, depending on the depth of the prompts.

Secondly, ask one person from each group to remain behind, whilst the other group members move to the next group. When they do this, the remaining person shares their thinking, and the incoming participants share theirs. At this point the flip chart paper should have two considerations written. This should take around five minutes.

Now, each group is provided with the second stage of the case study, problem or narrative. Again, they consider the topic, consider the questions and write their responses on the paper (ten minutes). Following this, again one person remains whilst the others move to the next table. As in the last case, the new group adds their standpoint, and their answers, to the questions.

Repeat the rotation.

The last stage is identical. Each new group reads the third stage of the issue at hand, discusses it and answers the questions, writing their responses and ideas on the flip chart paper. Again, a member remains whilst the others move to the next table, listens to the perspective of the preceding group and adds their point of view.

Repeat the rotation.

At the conclusion, there should be some large pieces of paper full of responses from the participants. If there is time, it can be helpful to hand these around the room and to invite the whole group to read them or to photograph them. Ideally, they would also make additions or clarifications to them as they read them.

Given the complexity of this exercise, the following offers an example where the *World Café* would work well. It contains a narrative about a freshly graduated PhD student and asks the participants to consider the situation from three different perspectives.

Case Study: Peter – Stage One

A very recent PhD graduate – Peter – has been hired on a short-term contract to teach a subject (at the same university where he did his PhD) which he knows very little about. The faculty appears to be a little desperate or they wouldn't have taken the risk of appointing someone in these circumstances. Peter needs the money, so agrees to do the work, which is only for one semester. He hopes that 'getting a foot in the door' will be helpful if any more permanent positions become available in the next year. He agrees to do the work two weeks prior to the start of the semester, after being personally approached by the Dean. He assumed that he would be provided with a full set of lecture notes, a complete and functioning LMS site, and an up-to-date unit guide. When these are not sent in the week prior to the start of the semester, Peter makes a polite enquiry to the Dean and is told that there are no materials, and that part of the workload is to organise all this material.

How would Peter feel? Why?
What should he do next?
How should he get ready for the start of the semester?

Stage Two

Peter starts the semester with a relatively heavy teaching load – which is good financially, but hard work as he prepares the subject material week by week. Never having taught before, the demands seem very high and his confidence levels are relatively low. In fact, he feels close to panic a good deal of the time. When challenged by students about the material, for example, Peter finds it difficult to answer them in a manner which seems to him to be authoritative and clear. In fact, because he's not teaching in his area of expertise, often he simply doesn't know the answer. One day Peter bumps into his PhD supervisor and tells her his story, sharing his low levels of confidence and self-esteem. His supervisor is very surprised by this given Peter's excellent academic record and his customary optimism and cheerfulness.

How much responsibility does his PhD supervisor have towards Peter?
What should his supervisor advise Peter to do?
Should the supervisor approach the Dean?

Stage Three

Peter finally reaches the end of the semester, and is glad it's over, although he's largely enjoyed the contact with students. He worked extremely hard, doing many, many (unpaid) hours of preparation work. The students' evaluations are in and, despite all Peter's efforts, he finds that he received relatively low marks which are below the faculty average. The students commented that Peter seemed 'unprepared', that he 'didn't know the subject matter', that he was 'disorganised'. Peter finds this not only hurtful, but unfair. He is also aware that these evaluations will be very important in gaining a teaching contract or a permanent position. As a result, Peter feels that all the work he put into his PhD in the hope of getting a permanent academic position was a waste of time. He also feels as if he has failed miserably as a teacher, despite all his work in helping students with their assessment, answering phone calls and emails quickly and efficiently and participating fully in all the online learning activities. Close to collapse, Peter gets angry and decides to go to the Dean to complain.

If, as the Dean, a staff member brought these student evaluations to you and described the context within which they were produced, what would you say?
What would your duty of care towards Peter be in these circumstances?
What actions should you take?

The *World Café* can also be a very successful and flexible tool for checking and revising understanding. If this exercise is used in the way Farr (2013) suggests, it can be a powerful confidence-building way to collaboratively revise the material from a subject prior to a final assessment. If used in this context, a relatively simple methodology can be employed – simply chunk sections of the curriculum into three, and ask students to brainstorm them. If this is used, the questions can be omitted, if this seems appropriate. Again, the participants move around the room adding material to each question posed, or each topic named. The results can be usefully captured on phones or whatever else is at hand, and used as a collaborative revision tool.

Conclusion

Whilst there is no general, agreed-upon term used for learning strategies which draw on the expertise and critical thinking of the students as well as the teacher, there is little doubt that what here are termed 'collaborative' teaching strategies are increasingly being used in higher education settings in the United Kingdom, Australia, New Zealand and the United States.

There are five main reasons for this move away from the traditional teaching model in which a body of knowledge is ideally transmitted intact from teacher to student with the success of such a transmission tested in a final exam.

Firstly, perhaps as a result of the demographic and economic shifts which led to the international widening participation strategy discussed in chapter 1, modern universities have moved away from viewing students as passive, receptive bodies. Contemporary higher education classrooms are – for the most part – full of students from diverse cultural backgrounds and of different ages who all bring a particular subjective standpoint to bear on the curriculum. Actively, and collaboratively, engaging students in learning activities enables them to bring this subjective standpoint, and their prior knowledge, to the matters at hand. This is seen as important because it leads to better learning outcomes for students, but it also prepares them to become lifelong learners. Moreover, the active use of students' experiences and perspectives in classrooms better equips them to deal competently with the diverse perspectives they are likely to meet in society throughout their lives.

Secondly, knowledge has become democratised, being more contestable since there are multitudinous sources of knowledge of all varieties made accessible by the Internet, emerging not only from universities, but from non-government organisations, charities, think tanks, research institutes, policy institutes, blogs, Facebook pages, Wikipedia and international organisations such as the OECD, amongst many others. In this context, twenty-first-century students are adept at researching online, used to contesting knowledges, and uncomfortable about the passive acceptance of data or theory without fully engaging with it. In part, these habits of mind have been developed at secondary schools which, over the last forty years, have been much more experimental and reformist about pedagogy than tertiary institutions (see Hattie 2009, for example). Confronted, when they arrive at university, with 'stand and deliver' teaching, they can very quickly become disengaged. Indeed, many of the pedagogies outlined here have been drawn and adapted from those used in secondary education.

Thirdly, to thrive in diverse societies such as ours, graduates need to have the capacities to interact easily with different perspectives, and to tackle complex national and international challenges using collaborative methods which generate carefully thought-out, long-term solutions. As discussed in chapter 1, the drive to rapidly increase the proportional number of graduates worldwide is precisely in order to ensure that greater numbers of citizens have these qualities. Collaborative learning strategies develop these skills – the ability to think critically, to analyse problems from multiple points of view and to work effectively with others whose standpoints differ from one's own. This discrete skill is further developed through the Critical Thinking strategies in chapter 6.

Fourthly, as discussed earlier, these qualities are those desired by employers. Without these 'soft' skills, graduates will face much greater challenges in the workplace than those with them. Whilst tertiary education has traditionally prepared students with the knowledge base with which to approach a career – whether it be in law, teaching, engineering, the creative arts, nursing or social policy – it now also needs to equip graduates with the skills which graduate attributes also make a claim for.

Finally, and most importantly, there is little evidence – after over fifty years of research – that teachers can transmit a body of knowledge to students effectively without actively engaging them. This, it seems, was understood in the secondary sector long before it was in the tertiary sector. All learners (no matter what their age) will match new information to that which they already know. When you allow them to do this in class – to recognise, match, test, evaluate – their critical thinking and absorption of new material increase dramatically. This is why collaborative teaching methods work.

Note

1 I'm extremely grateful to Jim Donohue for introducing me to this exercise when we were team teaching. It originated in an American comedy show from the 1970s.

Bibliography

Allen, S. (2008) '"Warming" the climate for learning', *The Teaching Professor* 22(2): 1.
Aronson, E. & S. Patnoe (2011) *Cooperation in the Classroom: The Jigsaw Method*, London: Pinter and Martin.
Braxton, J.M., W.A. Jones, A.S. Hirschy & H.V. Hartley (2008) 'The role of active learning in college student persistence', *New Directions for Teaching and Learning* 115: 71–83.
Braxton, J.M., J.F. Milem & A.S. Sullivan (2000) 'The influence of active learning on the college student departure process: Towards a revision of Tinto's theory', *The Journal of Higher Education* 71(5): 567–590.
Brown, J. (2002) *The World Café: A Resource Guide for Hosting Conversations That Matter*, Mill Valley, CA: Whole Systems Associates.
Brown, J. & D. Isaacs (2005) *The World Café: Shaping Our Futures through Conversations That Matter*, San Francisco, CA: Berrett-Koehler.
Chowning, J.T. (2009) 'Socratic seminars in science class', *Science Teacher* 76(7): 36–41.
Custer, H., J. Donohue, L.B. Hale, C. Hall, E. Hiatt, G. Kroesch & S. Valdez (2011) *AVID Postsecondary: Strategies for Success*, San Diego, CA: AVID Press.
Davidson, N., C.H. Major & L.K. Michaelsen (2014) 'Small-group learning in higher education – cooperative, collaborative, problem-based, and team-based learning: An introduction by the guest editors', *Journal on Excellence in College Teaching* 25(3–4): 1–6.
Davies, M. & A. Sinclair (2014) 'Socratic questioning in the Paideia Method to encourage dialogical discussions', *Research Papers in Education* 29(1): 20–43.
De Hei, M.A., J. Strijbos, E. Sjoer & W. Admiraal (2015) 'Collaborative learning in higher education: Lecturers' practices and beliefs', *Research Papers in Education* 30(2): 232–247.
Farr, J. (2013) '"Shared listening": Using the World Café approach as a revision tool in a final year undergraduate programme', *Compass: The Journal of Learning and Teaching at the University of Greenwich*.
Gaunt, H. & H. Westerlund (eds) (2013) *Collaborative Learning in Higher Music Education*, Farnham: Ashgate.
Goodin, H.J. & D. Stein (2008) 'Deliberative discussion as an innovative teaching strategy', *Journal of Nursing Education* 47(6): 272–274.
Hattie, J. (2009) *Visible Learning. A Synthesis of over 800 Meta-Analyses Relating to Achievement*, London: Routledge.
Hourigan, K. (2013) 'Increasing student engagement in large classes: The ARC model of application, response, and collaboration', *Teaching Sociology* 41(4): 353–359.
Johnson, D.W. & R.T. Johnson (2009) 'An educational psychology success story: Social interdependence theory and cooperative learning', *Educational Researcher* 38(5): 365–379.
Kingsley, P. (2011) 'The Socratic dialogue in asynchronous online discussions: Is constructivism redundant?', *Campus-Wide Information Systems* 28(5): 320–330.
Lanqin, Z., H. Ronghuai, H. Gwo-Jen & Y. Kaicheng (2015) 'Measuring knowledge elaboration based on a computer-assisted knowledge map analytical approach to collaborative learning', *Journal of Educational Technology & Society* 18(1): 321–336.

Lovejoy, S. (1988) 'How to zap your problems: Synectics – A problem solving technique for psychologists and teachers', *Educational Psychology in Practice* 3(4): 44–46.

Michaelsen, L.K., A.B. Knight & L.D. Fink (eds) (2002) *Team Based Learning: A Transformative Use of Small Groups in College Teaching*, Westport, CT: Greenwood Publishing Group.

Mitchell, S. (2006) 'Socratic dialogue, the humanities and the art of the question', *Arts & Humanities in Higher Education* 5(2): 181–197.

Persell, C.H., K.M. Pfeiffer & A. Syed (2008) 'How sociological leaders teach: Some key principles', *Teaching Sociology* 36(2): 108–124.

Popov, V., H.A. Biemans, A.N. Kuznetso & M. Mulder (2014) 'Use of an interculturally enriched collaboration script in computer-supported collaborative learning in higher education', *Technology, Pedagogy & Education* 23(3): 349–374.

Read, B., L. Archer & C. Leathwood (2003) 'Challenging cultures? Student conceptions of "belonging" and "isolation" at a post-1992 university', *Studies in Higher Education* 28(3): 261–277.

Richardson, S. & A. Radloff (2014) 'Allies in learning: Critical insights into the importance of staff–student interactions in university education', *Teaching in Higher Education* 19(6): 603–615.

Roberts, S. (2011) 'Traditional practice for non-traditional students? Examining the role of pedagogy in higher education retention', *Journal of Further and Higher Education* 35(2): 183–199.

Roberts, T. & L. Billings (1999) *The Paideia Classroom: Teaching for Understanding*, New York: Eye on Education.

Tangalakis, K., K. Hughes, C. Brown & K. Dickson (2014) 'The use of explicit teaching strategies for academic staff and students in science foundation subjects', *International Journal of Innovation in Science and Mathematics Education* 22(3): 42–51.

Tapp, J. (2014) '"I actually listened, I'm proud of myself": The effects of a participatory pedagogy on students' constructions of academic identities', *Teaching in Higher Education* 19(4): 323–335.

Tekbiyik, A. (2015) 'The use of jigsaw collaborative learning method in teaching socioscientific issues: The case of nuclear energy', *Journal of Baltic Science Education* 14(2): 237–253.

Thompson, K.J., B. Switky & A. Gilinsky (2012) 'Impromptu presentations: Boosting student learning and engagement through spontaneous collaboration', *Journal of Education for Business* 87(1): 14–21.

Tredway, L. (1995) 'Socratic seminars: Engaging students in intellectual discourse', *Educational Leadership* 53(1): 26–29.

Chapter 6

Thinking critically

Introduction

The ability to think critically, alongside the ability to work collaboratively, is ubiquitous in universities' claims for their graduates' skill set. In contemporary universities, then, there is an expectation that critical thinking skills will be developed by students – but largely without being specifically taught how to do this (Buckley *et al*. 2015; Lewine *et al*. 2015; Moon 2008). This is not universally true, with many disciplines purposefully teaching critical thinking skills to their students in diverse ways (see Buskist & Irons 2008; Franklin *et al*. 2014; Howard *et al*. 2015; Oyler & Romanelli 2014; Zare & Mukundan 2015 for examples).

The argument has been convincingly mounted by Fisher (2011) and others that the development of critical thinking skills should not be left to osmosis, but should be taught explicitly to higher education students. Largely this is because of the move away from the passive 'banking' concept of knowledge transferral (Freire 2000) towards one where the conceptual, analytical and problem-solving skills are perceived of as equally important as the material under consideration.

This is not a new proposition. John Dewey, an early-twentieth-century American educator, philosopher and psychologist, was one of the first to consider and develop the notion of critical thinking as a self-reflective, active, purposeful endeavour. He defined it as:

> Active, persistent, and careful consideration of a belief or supposed form of knowledge in the light of the grounds which support it and the further conclusions to which it trends.
>
> (Dewey 1909: 9)

This is a relatively simple and succinct description of what Dewey in fact called 'reflective thinking'. Yet it contains within it the key concepts which permeate even contemporary thinking about this.

Firstly, the learner is an active participant in the process, and not simply subjected to what might be called a 'knowledge dump'. The learner doesn't learn from someone else imparting information, but enquires, poses questions and finds the answers to their questions independently, or in collaboration with other learners as discussed in chapter 5.

Secondly, the notions of persistence and carefulness invoke the idea that the learner employs reason to adjudicate, for example, between competing sets of evidence. Exploring the credibility levels for rival points of view and the evidence propositions they employ become the key means through which a scholarly hypothesis or a scholarly conclusion can be formed (Jenkins *et al.* 2015; Moon 2008; Smith 2011; Zare & Mukundan 2015). The ability to confidently participate in such a process involves a complex set of skills which can, and should, be explicitly taught to students in order that they have a metacognitive understanding of the learning process.

Thirdly, Dewey suggests here that the critical thinking process enables one not only to assess the credibility of evidence but also to extrapolate from this evidence. Using higher-order thinking the learner should be in a position to predict or hypothesise what further implications might follow from both the evidence, and the reasoned position which the learner has arrived at.

This is a simple account of the foundation of critical thinking, and an argument for its use. Critical thinking is also a discrete discipline area itself, a growing area of interest within Philosophy (see Bowell & Kemp 2002; hooks 2010; Horvath & Forte 2011; Nosich 2012; Wright 2001), whilst also enjoying broad appeal with the general public as a useful way in which to engage with the world (see Cohen 2015; Jones 2009; Kahneman 2011; Kaller 2014).

But what do we mean precisely when we discuss critical thinking skills? There are a set of principles associated with critical thinking skills, many of which will be familiar given that they're apparent in many of the teaching strategies discussed earlier.

Firstly, and simply, there is a willingness to engage openly with the learning process, and a commitment to test ideas or hypotheses and to change or adapt the hypothesis as a result. Such willingness may not happen spontaneously in a classroom, but it can be generated when the learning environment feels safe. The teaching strategies discussed in chapter 3 are instrumental to creating trust and mutual respect in order that students feel secure enough to be open to new ideas, and to testing them.

Secondly, critical thinking should involve and increase the learners' ability to distinguish between different viewpoints, and to engage productively with those viewpoints. In essence this means more than being able to sympathise, it means to empathise and to have the capacity to interact with multiple perspectives. Teaching through explicitly developing, and rewarding, this skill by using some of the following strategies will greatly assist.

The third principle involves a sense of disruption. We are all disrupted when we learn something new, particularly when a standpoint has been shifted as a result. Amsler (2014) goes further and suggests that pedagogies of 'encounter' and 'discomfort' could, and should, be purposefully used in universities in order to enhance the learning process (p. 281). The reason for this is that it develops an acceptance of ambiguity and unpredictability which in turn leads to students' preparedness to make mistakes, to encounter and negotiate the unknowns, and to develop a robust scholarly disposition.

The fourth attribute which critical thinking assists in building is individual self-awareness. Further to the ability to interrogate the perspectives of others mentioned above, critical thinking also helps students understand their own responses to material and to assess their own views or standpoints, and their evidence base. This is a constructive way to improve students' levels of disinterest, and their independence from immediate responses to material. It develops reasoning skills. Having a high level of such self-awareness can also significantly change a learner's sense of self in order that they perceive themselves as a learner, even a scholar.

Fifth is the ability to use metacognition which, simply, is being in a position to think about thinking and knowing. Commonly thought of as a higher-order thinking skill, metacognition draws on all the features of critical thinking just discussed – to reason, to think independently, to distinguish between subject and object, to readily critically confront new information and so forth. It is also the basis from where one can start to review abstract concepts and to synthesise them with new material.

Finally, and most importantly, critical thinking helps people to develop the ability to clearly articulate and present ideas to others. Partly this is due to the process of understanding precisely how a conclusion was reached – once the learner knows this they can step another through that process of reasoning, and to their conclusion. If their audience presents an alternative conclusion, they are in a position to confront it and process it.

The following teaching strategies and tools are useful in supporting the development of critical thinking. Some should be consistently used as a means of framing the class; others should be used less frequently and for specific purposes. They are all suitable for use across diverse disciplines.

1 Essential Question

Widely used in primary and high schools, the essential question is also appropriate for the tertiary environment. Its purpose is twofold:

- It informs the students about the week's topic by clearly demonstrating what it is they should be in a position to confidently answer by the end of the class.
- It enables the teacher to check at the end of the class how close to answering the question they are. This can equally also be done halfway though to provide the group with a signal about their progress.

When building an essential question, it is important to use higher-order thinking, asking the students to evaluate, generalise, imagine, judge, predict, hypothesise, speculate or forecast (see pp. 119–120 for more on question levels). Asking, for example, a question which merely requests a non-negotiable factual response cannot assist in the developing of the critical thinking skills discussed earlier.

Essential questions can fall into any of the following four question styles:

- **Probing consequences** – with these, learners are to contemplate the results or repercussions of their suppositions and concepts. One example might be *If (a particular approach) is taken, what would be the outcome?*
- **Probing assumptions** – these questions ask students to consider the assumptions or the beliefs which form the basis of their argument. It enables them to unpack their reasoning processes and the ways in which they arrived at their conclusion. One example might be *Can you tell me why...?*
- **Probing evidence** – this question style requires a learner to provide an explanation for the concept under consideration. They can be used to interrogate the reasoning and logic behind their suppositions. One example might be *Can you provide evidence for...?*
- **Clarification** – these support learners to examine why a question is being asked, or the reasoning providing the foundation for an idea or an opinion. Clarification questions typically require the learner to produce an explanation. One example might be *Why do you believe that...?*

Once the question has been built, display it at the start of the lecture or tutorial and ask the students to spend two minutes writing their response to the question. Then, at the conclusion, display the question again and ask them to respond to it again. This is useful in order that they are able to perceive the movement of their knowledge base and, importantly, their thinking. If appropriate, provide the space for a general feedback session since it will enable the teacher to also check on the progress the class is making. If it appears to be too slow, this activity can be extended by asking them to work in pairs to generate a joint answer, and then having another general feedback session.

In short, essential questions can be a useful and time-efficient framing exercise which guides the students to understanding the purpose of the week's class, but also to some reflection on their personal progress towards an informed answer to the question.

2 Questioning Levels

This tool is one which can be used to specifically teach critical thinking skills. As such, it stands alone as an exercise insofar as its purpose is to teach questioning skills *per se* rather than to be used to wrap around curricula, although this can also be done if it's useful.

The argument for using purposeful, high-level questions in learning and teaching rests on the belief that the use of such questions guides thinking, stimulates discussion, focusses attention, facilitates a deeper level of learning and enables students' self-awareness as they come to understand how much they do (and don't) know (Carvalho-Grevious 2013; Davies & Sinclair 2014; Mitchell 2006; Tredway 1995). The notion of questioning as a key stimulant for learning is embedded in many of the teaching strategies in this book, so the development of questioning as a skill, and a tool, is extremely beneficial.

Perhaps the best-known longstanding model for ranking levels of cognition was developed in the 1950s by an educational psychologist called Benjamin Bloom and it is still used widely in the education sector at primary, secondary and sometimes also at tertiary levels (see Bloom 1984; Krathwohl 2002). Its resilience is partially a result of its simplicity (see Figure 6.1).

Beginning at the bottom of the triangle, then, Bloom argued that the most basic level of cognition is where one comprehends, and can repeat, discrete facts. For the purposes of building questions at this level, the following verbs will be found in writing prompts: define, arrange, state, repeat, order, list, duplicate and so forth. For use in a classroom discussion the focus should be on an understanding of the specific cognitive activity, which in this case is order and repetition. Consequently 'What is A?', 'Where is A?', and 'What came first, A or B?' are likely questions in this domain.

The second stratum 'understanding' involves more than simple recognition or repetition, it includes the ability to apply a critical perspective to the knowledge, to relate two pieces of knowledge and to classify like knowledges together. Generating questions using this cognition level for writing tasks would include words such as describe, select, express, translate, discuss, explain, classify, locate or indicate. In class, the aim is to use verbal questions which encourage students to make these links, and to be able to classify information sets. To this end, then, the following question styles would be used: 'How alike are A and B?', 'Do A and B belong together? Why?', 'How could you express A in another way?' and so on.

The third Bloom level moves beyond a fundamental understanding (or appreciation) of the material under consideration to an understanding of where it might

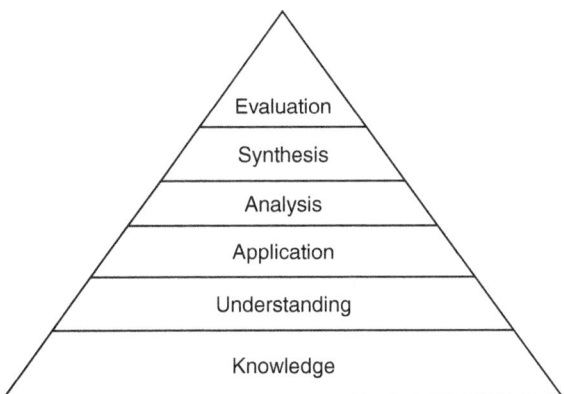

Figure 6.1 Bloom's hierarchy

be applied. In other words, the knowledge now known is related to something currently unknown and the interaction between the two is explored. This is effectively a middle level of cognition, so working within this area when building essay questions or questions for reports or any other assignment style, one would use the following key words: illustrate, solve, apply, demonstrate, interpret etc. Similarly, questions for use as an essential question for the week, as prompts for *Socratic Seminars* or simply as a discussion generator would follow a similar structure to 'How would A work with/in B?', 'What impact would A have on B and C?' or 'Could A be applied to B?'

Similar in complexity level, the fourth stratum 'analysis' pertains to breaking the object of enquiry into its component parts, being in the position to describe how they might relate to one another. At this level, it is accurate to claim that deeper thinking is being developed, as is critical thinking, since the metacognition levels involved go well beyond the first three levels. In writing prompts then, one would find: analyse, compare, contrast, distinguish, discuss, assess, critique. Verbally, one would find questions with arrangements such as 'How useful is A? Why?', 'Which is better, A or B? Why?' or 'What are the differences between A and B in terms of C?'

The penultimate stratum is labelled 'synthesis' and moves the learner away from the discrete object(s) of enquiry themselves, and towards high-level thinking which ultimately involves the learner in starting to hypothesise from the evidence base they have interrogated. At this level then, they are asked to think more creatively, and to extrapolate. Within this domain, assignment prompts would feature at least some of the following: construct, compose, design, develop, predict, formulate, propose. This is perhaps the simplest (and most enjoyable) level at which to construct challenging questions within the classroom since answering them involves both imagination and creativity. The following structures can be a beginning for building such questions: 'How could we design an improvement on A?', 'What would happen if we did A with B?', 'What will A look like in fifty years?', 'Can we create a complete alternative to A? What would it look like?' and so forth.

At the very top of Bloom's pyramid comes 'evaluation'. Here, the learner is positioned as having comprehended the foundational features of the topic, understanding it, knowing how it might be applied, understanding its constituent parts and how they interact with each other and being able to hypothesise about its likely development or its preferable alternative. The final stage, then, involves a fully informed appraisal and evaluation of the object of knowledge under consideration. As such, it draws on all the preceding stages of cognition and in effect completes them. If generating questions for assignments which are located at this level, the following verbs are valuable: assess, argue, defend, estimate, predict, judge, evaluate. Likewise, questions for use in class might look something like this: 'How useful is A?', 'What are A's disadvantages?', 'Which is better for A, B or C?', 'What would be the best outcome for A under the circumstances of B and C?' or 'Is A ultimately doomed? Why?' These questions facilitate drawing upon not only an understanding of the topic at hand, but also upon contrasting or complementary knowledge sets through which to make a judgement.

Thinking critically 119

The process of stepping through levels of understanding can be a powerful means to educate students about what learning is as an activity in itself, and to help them develop self-awareness of their own levels of understanding. To this end, it is valuable to use Bloom's taxonomy openly with classes, sharing where they might be at any point in the teaching period, and explicitly say that it is anticipated they will reach the top of the pyramid. Similarly, the typology can be used when constructing assessment rubrics for criteria-based assessment in which students responding to the writing prompt only using the first or second strata receive less reward than those using the sixth.

Another way in which to help students approach and understand Bloom's taxonomy is to use an exercise which explicitly steps them through the continuum from the lower to the higher levels. It is a relatively challenging exercise which takes approximately fifteen minutes to complete, but it is extremely effective, and collaborative.

It involves the use of a story which all the participants should reasonably be expected to know – a popular film, novel, play or even a fairy tale work well. A table should be built which requires students' responses. When constructing the table, divide it into three levels, grouping Bloom's taxonomy's levels in twos, and distribute it to the class in either hard or soft copy (see Table 6.1).

Then furnish the table using the plot from the chosen film, novel, play or fairy tale. In the example in Table 6.2, *Romeo and Juliet* has been used given that it is the most well-known story in the (Western) world.

Table 6.3 is another example, this time using topics commonly used in health sciences.

Table 6.4 is an example which might be used in a generic business subject.

Clearly, this format can be adapted to any discipline and any topic.

To use this strategy, the class can be divided into small groups where they take a row each and build one of the Level Two and Three questions. Equally, if time allows and it is appropriate, you can ask each small group to answer each of them, or two of them. Depending on the levels of cognition in the class, Level Two questions can be completed before moving to Level Three.

Table 6.1 Template for questioning levels

Level 1 (knowledge, understanding)	*Level 2 (application, analysis)*	*Level 3 (synthesis, evaluation)*

120 Thinking critically

Table 6.2 Example using *Romeo and Juliet*

Level 1 (knowledge, understanding)	Level 2 (application, analysis)	Level 3 (synthesis, evaluation)
What is Juliet's surname?	Why is her surname important?	What does the importance of her surname tell us about the society where the play is set?
How old is Juliet?		
Where is the play set?		
Whom is Juliet promised to in marriage?		
What does Friar Lawrence do?		
How does Juliet die?		

Table 6.3 Example from health education

Level 1 (knowledge, understanding)	Level 2 (application, analysis)	Level 3 (synthesis, evaluation)
What is stress?	What leads to stress?	Would it be possible for an individual in the Western world not to suffer stress?
How could motivation be defined?		
What is well-being?		
What is mental health?		
What are the perimeters of hypoglycaemia?		
How might chronic obstructive pulmonary disease be defined?		

When preparing the group to do this exercise, it is important to clearly emphasise that they are not to answer the questions, but to create two more which reflect the respective level at which they are working. This is not easy, and so it is useful to be available as they work through the exercise, providing guidance.

When they have all finished, display the table they were given and ask for their responses in a general feedback session. Commonly, students will confuse Level Two and Level Three question styles, and if this is the case, be continually explicit about the differences, and if there is confusion ask them to rephrase. This is relatively easy to do.

Table 6.4 Example from business education

Level 1 (knowledge, understanding)	Level 2 (application, analysis)	Level 3 (synthesis, evaluation)
What is accounting?	What does accounting enable us to do?	How would contemporary businesses function without accounting?
How can we define 'management'?		
What is marketing?		
What are the characteristics of an entrepreneur?		
When did contemporary business practices develop?		
How might ethical business practices be defined?		

Whilst at first glance, this might appear to be an onerous exercise, it can be extremely valuable in developing students' awareness of their own cognition levels and the ways in which they can, and should, be developed in order to become successful learners.

3 The Frayer Model

The eponymous Frayer Model is a graphic organiser created by Dorothy Frayer at the University of Wisconsin, originally to assist in the teaching of mathematical concepts to high school students (Frayer *et al.* 1969). It is, however, an extremely versatile visual teaching tool which can be used in a wide variety of disciplines. Its purpose is to assist students' development of knowledge about a concept, a theory or an object through drawing on prior knowledge and through contrasting the topic under investigation with examples and non-examples. It can be used for formative assessment at any point. It particularly contributes to developing clarity and contrast for concepts, theories or objects under discussion which are similar in their nature to other concepts, theories or objects which the students have come across. In so doing, the Frayer Model can develop conceptual understanding at the conclusion of a topic, when students' understanding has been developed. It has also been widely used to build vocabulary (Greenwood 2002), and can be used as an addition to the *Learning the Language* strategies 1 and 2 discussed in chapter 4, or at the beginning and at the end of a session in order that students can ascertain their growing understanding of a topic.

A blank Frayer model looks like Figure 6.2.

Each student should be provided with either a hard or soft copy, with the key term under interrogation provided in the central circle. Ask them to complete the model on their own, then in pairs.

122 Thinking critically

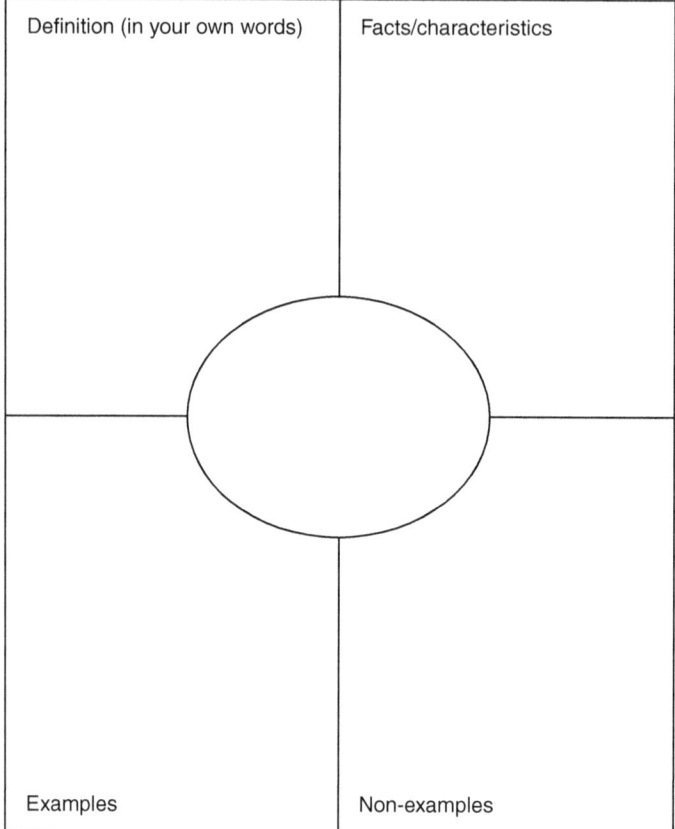

Figure 6.2 The Frayer Model

If using this strategy at the beginning of a class, there is no absolute need to feed back. If using it at the conclusion of a class, feeding back provides the opportunity for a knowledge check by both the students and the teacher.

Depending on the term in the central circle, this exercise can be done relatively quickly if it is used as a simple vocabulary clarification. If there is a complex concept, or theory, placed in the middle, then expect to spend ten or so minutes.

Frayer models can also be used as an interactive, collaborative revision tool at the conclusion of a teaching session. In order to do this, reproduce the model on a large sheet of paper (A2 or A3) and place the key terms which the class has explored in the middle of the model. Around six of these works well.

Place them at stations around the room, and invite the class to move from station to station, individually, in pairs or in small groups. As they move, they add to the Frayer model without repeating what others have already said. At the conclusion (after around twenty minutes) there should be six Frayer models which are comprehensively completed. Encourage the class to take photos of the models, which can later be used as an *aide-memoire*.

In terms of the time required to use the Frayer model as a whole-group exercise, around twenty minutes would be the norm.

4 Philosophical Chairs

Used widely as a teaching strategy to generate a disciplined debate, *Philosophical Chairs* is similar in its tone to the *Socratic Seminar* discussed on p. 103 insofar as it explicitly teaches students to (potentially) adopt a position on a topic contrary to their own beliefs and to argue for that position using evidence (Nicholson-Preuss 2013). There are many variations available for use, but here the simplest version will be described (see Barkley *et al.* 2014).

It is a scaffolded exercise which enables participants to develop their position and the available evidence for it on their own, then with a partner, then with half the class. Like the other exercises with this formation, this enables students to rehearse their thinking and discussion points before they become engaged in a public debate. As such, it is equally beneficial for those with low confidence levels, as well as those with higher levels of self-assurance.

It also develops students' critical thinking skills insofar as they are engaged in assembling an argument that they may well not agree with. It invites them to adopt a disinterested position, and to formulate a case for its veracity. In so doing, they are able to practise many of the skills central to critical thinking which were discussed at the start of the chapter, and which are central to scholarly activities in general.

Through participating in *Philosophical Chairs* they:

1   Engage openly with the learning process
2   Increase their ability to distinguish between different viewpoints, and to engage productively with those viewpoints
3   Experience a sense of disruption as their position on a topic or statement is revised through debate
4   Build individual self-awareness about their viewpoint and in doing so
5   Develop their metacognition and
6   Acquire the ability to clearly articulate and present ideas to others

Philosophical Chairs is best put to use in order to consider a piece of text, a film, a website or even an image. Be clear that the expectation is that they will come to class familiar with the reading or other object under discussion.

As a prompt, it is crucial to build a statement (rather than a question) to be discussed during the *Philosophical Chairs* debate. In so doing, ensure that the statement is dichotomous (contains a clear 'yes' and 'no' division, in other words) and that it has the capacity to engage the students both intellectually and emotionally, if that is possible. Without a strong engagement with the statement, the debate will lack energy and, therefore, impact.

Some typical examples of such statements might be:

- Humans should stop eating animals
- Juries should be abolished
- People who do not fully vaccinate their children should be unable to enrol them in school
- We should increase the number of chimpanzees used to test new pharmaceuticals
- We should double our overseas aid budget
- Governments should have a quota of women
- ADHD is a condition used to disguise poor parenting

Choose a statement which is discipline-specific, and pertinent to the topic under consideration for the week. The key considerations are that it is pertinent and dichotomous.

Display the prompt, and ask them to spend five minutes, on their own, writing their immediate response to the statement, and the reasons they have for that response.

On completion, ask them to pair with someone close by, and to share their responses with one another. This should take in the region of five minutes.

As a means of recording where the group as a whole sits along a continuum of 'yes' and 'no' before the debate begins, draw a line on the whiteboard and ask the class to record their position along that line. This can be done by simply placing a cross on the line with a whiteboard marker (this is anonymous). Equally, sticky notes with symbols or names can be used. At the conclusion of the debate, they will be asked to revisit the line, and to move their cross or their sticky note if they have revised their viewpoint. If the debate goes well, many do, and this is a useful visual record of the group's development of their critical thinking skills.

Once completed, it is time to split the group into two. The simplest way to undertake this is to number them – one, two, one, two – until each participant has a number, and a group. Ask the two groups to meet, and to spend approximately ten minutes building their argument either for or against the statement. When doing this, it is beneficial to encourage them to use the Internet in order that they have data to hand. Suggest that at this point they collect a number of talking points they can put to use during the debate. This provides a shared resource base, and relieves each individual from the need and pressure to generate arguments alone – something which can be very challenging for introverted students.

At this point, ask them to stand in a row facing one another with the 'ones' facing the 'twos'. Ensure that there is enough physical space for this to take place easily, and that your students do not have significant mobility issues. If so, *Philosophical Chairs* can equally be undertaken with the class still facing one another, but sitting down.

There are a set of helpful rules of engagement for this exercise which should be displayed for, and understood by, the participants:

- Each side should speak one after the other.
- Each side should listen to the other's point of view.

- They should speak one at a time.
- They should paraphrase what the previous speaker said – their key points – and respond to it.
- They should use the protocol whereby two people (on their side) mount an argument before they speak again.

Commonly, these protocols will be broken (initially) as participants slowly become familiarised with the purpose of the process, and the process itself. If so, it is important to intervene in order to guide the session. Be clear about what is occurring, and why it is ultimately unhelpful. This is not always a smooth process, with some awkwardness and self-consciousness commonly apparent. If it is, acknowledge openly what is happening, explaining that they will shortly feel more comfortable as they become more accustomed to the protocols.

A typical scenario occurs when two combatants attempt to dominate the debate. Simply intervene, explaining the importance of sharing and collaboration. Reiterate the convention whereby participants from each side speak in turn, and restate that there must be two people who speak before each individual can speak again. This protocol quashes the dominance by particular personalities, and engenders a collaborative, critical endeavour which enables most class members to purposefully participate for the benefit of everyone.

It is a matter of judgement about when to conclude the *Philosophical Chairs* session. This is best done simply by listening to the volume level, and ascertaining when the participants have reached the conclusion of their thinking and their arguments. A key to this is whether or not the participants begin to repeat points which have already been made. Similarly, they may well move on from the topic to tell anecdotes, in which case, point this out, keeping them on topic, on evidence and on point. If the volume dies down or if repetition begins – then terminate the session.

At the conclusion, it can be productive to ask the participants to return to the whiteboard and to change the position of their cross or their sticky note, which declared where they sat on the continuum between 'yes' and 'no' at the start of the session.

Following this, ask them to write a short position paper, as they did at the start of the exercise, which summarises where they now stand in relation to the prompt statement. How significantly has their point of view changed?

When this has been completed, conduct an evaluation of the process with the class, asking the following questions:

- Was their individual point of view altered? By how much? What was the pivotal point for change?
- How did they feel arguing a point of view which they did not necessarily agree with?
- What evidence did they draw upon?
- How do they think the class might improve upon the exercise – in terms of their adherence to the *Philosophical Chairs* protocols?
- Would they like to make any changes for next time?

126 Thinking critically

Like the other teaching strategies outlined in this chapter, *Philosophical Chairs* typically is extremely engaging and, under analysis, enables students to productively engage with the learning process, with metacognition and, ultimately, their own sense of their developing levels of critical thinking.

It is a relatively time-consuming but valuable process which typically occupies around one hour of time. It does, however, generate deep thinking and critical thinking, which will stay with the participants. It facilitates disciplined debate, reasoned argument and the ability of students to step outside what might begin as a subjective, personalised domain to one which is evidence- and argument-based (adapted from Custer *et al.* 2011).

5 Graphic Organisers

Graphic Organisers are essentially diagrams, symbolic representations, which can be used to assist students to dismantle a concept, a historical event, an organ, a chemical process, a legal problem or anything else pertinent to the week's topic. They can be used in any discipline for this purpose. For visual learners, these are very useful tools for helping students to develop metacognitive understanding about a topic or a number of linked topics. It also helps them to be in a position to disassemble and reassemble the component parts of a concept or theory (Custer *et al.* 2011).

As such, they are similar in intent to the mind map discussed by Ferrand *et al.* (2002), but can be built using a number of online applications, software or simply in hard copy to begin with. Equally useful are the SmartArt and Chart facilities in MS *Word*. These can be approached as graphic organisers which relate to the three levels of cognition and questioning discussed earlier insofar as level one organisers simply facilitate the laying out of a series of facts or points of interest with little focus on the relationship between the points of interest. Some examples follow.

The simple linear model shown in Figure 6.3 can be used for a cause and effect continuum.

The model shown in Figure 6.4 links ideas or topics placed in the upper tier, with sub-topics or sub-ideas placed in the bottom tier. It also facilitates the arrangement of linked topics or ideas laterally.

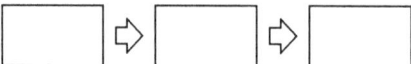

Figure 6.3 Simple linear model

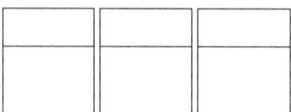

Figure 6.4 Topics with sub-topics (or examples) beneath

Thinking critically 127

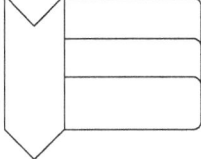

Figure 6.5 Topic with sub-topics (or examples) listed to the right

In Figure 6.5, one central idea, theme or topic is displayed on the left, with the resulting ideas, themes or topics listed on the right.

Second-level graphic organisers are designed to set out relationships between things. Similar to the Frayer Model discussed earlier, they are designed to display the relationships between hierarchical components, whilst also showing the connections between each component in the hierarchy, and offering the possibility of adding explanatory text via the external text boxes.

In the example in Figure 6.6, a centrifugal idea can be placed at the centre, with four secondary topics following it, then four more.

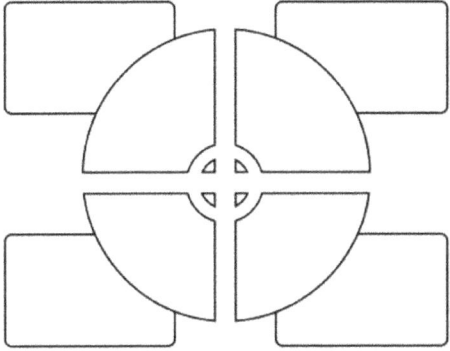

Figure 6.6 Hierarchical graphic organiser

The organiser in Figure 6.7 also displays hierarchy and connection between multiple parts, with the bottom row of hexagons forming the lowest part of the hierarchy and the top row forming the top. Again, explanatory text can be installed into the text boxes, and the organiser can be expanded or reduced according to need.

The example in Figure 6.8 provides an indication of a timeline, an indication of significance and (implicitly) an indication of hierarchy whereby significant events, or reactions, are attached to the large, empty circles and resulting events or reactions attached to the smaller circles. This could be used for any topic requiring a series of events to be placed in an order.

Level-three graphic organisers facilitate the extension of the material covered – linking it not only to prior knowledge, but to additional material outside of the class. They also enable students to build a more complex model which can relate a much higher number of items, facts or points of interest.

128 Thinking critically

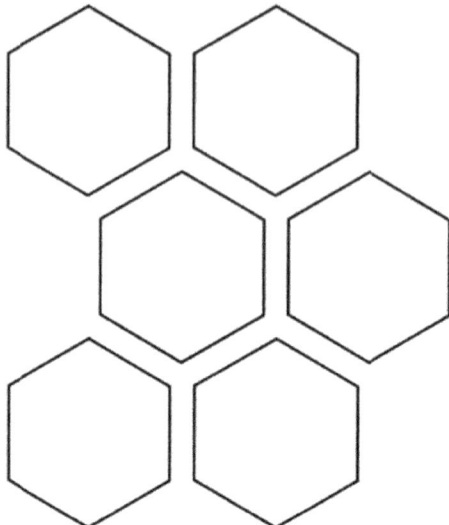

Figure 6.7 Hierarchical graphic organiser with multiple parts

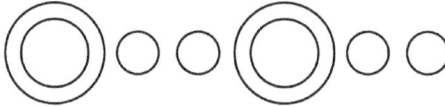

Figure 6.8 Timeline graphic organiser

Figure 6.9 is essentially a Venn diagram which can be used simply to extend, to add effects and so on.

Commonly known as 'mind maps' (Ferrand *et al.* 2002), the two models shown in Figure 6.10 and Figure 6.11 can accommodate multiple sets of data and range from the very simple format illustrated immediately below, to one with much greater levels of complexity. As such it is infinitely variable.

There are many other models available, and the above are simply examples of the ways in which such models can be put to use as a formative or a summative exercise whereby students are invited to think critically, and to display their thinking in a graphic form.

If this teaching strategy is chosen, use the 1-2-4 formation used for some of the earlier exercises. Here, students complete the graphic organiser on their own, initially, but then they compare and contrast their results with one other person. Each can amend, revise or complete their model at this stage. On completion, each pair joins another and the above process is repeated.

When the noise level in the room starts to dwindle, it is safe to assume that the class has completed the exercise. It can be helpful at this stage for the teacher to offer the class an exemplar graphic organiser, to explicitly step through the

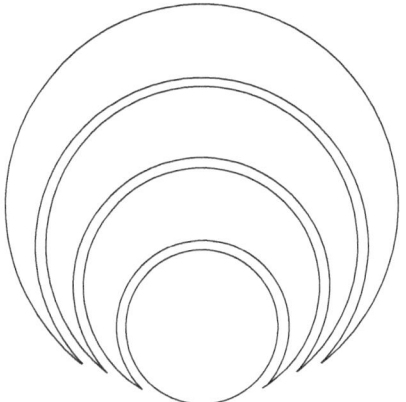

Figure 6.9 Sequential graphic organiser

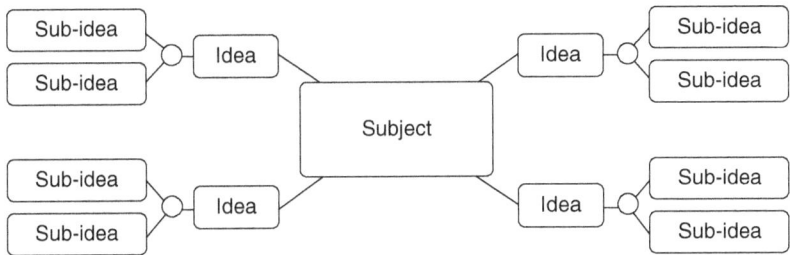

Figure 6.10 Mind map 1

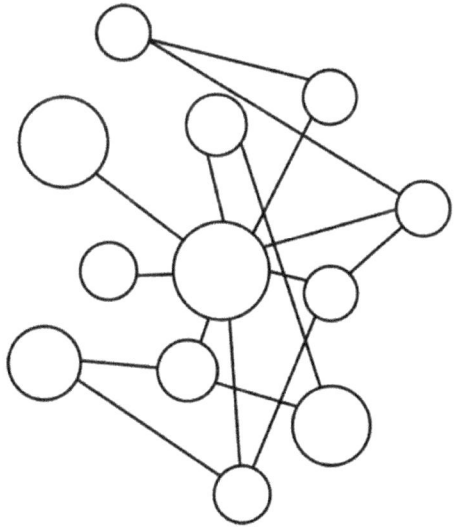

Figure 6.11 Mind map 2

building of the model and the thought processes which preceded it. Be prepared for feedback from the whole group, and the possible need to make adjustments to the model if you are persuaded by their arguments, or if a point has been missed.

Equally, a convincing graphic organiser produced by one of the small groups can be used effectively as a demonstration model. If this method is chosen, ensure that it is an excellent model, without many additions or revisions required in order that the authors feel fully supported in presenting their work to the whole group.

Graphic organisers are potentially the most positivist activity discussed in this chapter insofar as they are about order and hierarchy, rather than about discussion and debate. Nevertheless, debate will be had about relative hierarchical positions, and in so doing, students will be engaged in collaborative learning and in critical thinking.

Conclusion

The chapter began with the claim that the imperative for any learner to develop the ability to think critically was established as far back as early in the twentieth century (Dewey 1909), and has more recently become a key feature of the qualities which both universities and workplaces expect graduates to have. It was also argued that to increase the speed at which these qualities are adopted, they should be taught explicitly rather than expecting students to develop them through osmosis. The point about this, is that some students will, and some students will not, which will largely be determined by the levels of educational and cultural capital they bring with them when they enter the university. Socially inclusive educators, then, tend towards the use of the teaching strategies outlined above since they leave nothing to chance, with students having a clear understanding of the need for critical skills, and some expertise in their use.

It is anticipated that with the careful, purposeful insertion of the teaching strategies discussed previously, it should be possible to assist students – from whatever social and cultural background – to acquire a set of skills which will be of great value throughout their lives as students, and beyond. Through using them, they should be in a position to: engage with (and test) ideas; be able to distinguish between different viewpoints and assess their credibility; change their views; acquire self-awareness of their standpoint and their reasons for holding it which moves beyond belief or feeling; have a level of metacognition in order that they might both understand the process of learning, and understand their own levels of learning; and, finally, they should be able to clearly articulate and present a reasoned argument.

Bibliography

Amsler, S. (2014) '"By ones and twos and tens": Pedagogies of possibility for democratising higher education', *Pedagogy, Culture and Society* 22(2): 275–294.

Barkley, E.F., C.H. Major & K.P. Cross (2014) *Collaborative Learning Techniques. A Handbook for College Faculty*, San Francisco, CA: Jossey-Bass.

Bloom, B. (1984) *Taxonomy of Educational Objectives*, Boston, MA: Allyn and Bacon.
Bowell, T., & G. Kemp (2002) *Critical Thinking. A Concise Guide*, London: Taylor & Francis.
Buckley, J., M. Hargraves, W. Trochim & T. Archibald (2015) 'Defining and teaching evaluative thinking: Insights from research on critical thinking', *American Journal of Evaluation* 36(3): 375–388.
Buskist, W. & J. Irons (2008) 'Simple strategies for teaching.' In D.S. Dunn, J.S. Halonen, and R.A. Smith (eds), *Teaching Critical Thinking in Psychology: A Handbook of Best Practice*, Oxford: Wiley-Blackwell, pp. 49–57.
Carvalho-Grevious, M. (2013) 'Breaking the cycle of shame: Socratic teaching methods to enhance critical thinking', *Journal of Baccalaureate Social Work* 18(S1): 77–94.
Cohen, M. (2015) *Critical Thinking Skills for Dummies*, Chichester: John Wiley.
Custer, H.H., J. Donohue, L.B. Hale, C. Hall, E. Hiatt, G. Kroesch, B. Krohn, S. Malik, F. Muhammad, V. Quijano, D. Shapiro & S. Valdez (2011) *AVID Postsecondary Strategies for Success*, San Diego, CA: AVID Press.
Davies, M. & A. Sinclair (2014) 'Socratic questioning in the Paideia Method to encourage dialogical discussions', *Research Papers in Education* 29(1): 20–43.
Dewey, J. (1909) *Moral Principles in Education*, Boston, MA: Houghton Mifflin.
Ferrand, P., F. Hussain & E. Hennessy (2002) 'The efficacy of the mind map study technique', *Medical Education* 36(5): 426–431.
Fisher, A. (2011) *Critical Thinking: An Introduction* (2nd ed), Cambridge: Cambridge University Press.
Franklin, D., J. Weinberg & J. Reifler (2014) 'Teaching writing and critical thinking in large political science classes', *Journal of Political Science Education* 10(2): 155–165.
Frayer, D., W.C. Frederick & H.J. Klausmeier (1969) *A Schema for Testing the Level of Cognitive Mastery*, Madison, WI: Wisconsin Center for Education Research.
Freire, P. (2000) *Pedagogy of the Oppressed*, New York: Continuum.
Greenwood, S.C. (2002) 'Making words matter: Vocabulary study in the content areas', *The Clearing House: A Journal of Educational Strategies, Issues and Ideas* 75(5): 258–263.
hooks, b. (2010) *Teaching Critical Thinking. Practical Wisdom*, New York: Routledge.
Horvath, C.P. & J.M. Forte (2011) *Critical Thinking*, Hauppauge, NY: Nova Science Publishers.
Howard, L., T. Tang & M. Jill Austin (2015) 'Teaching critical thinking skills: Ability, motivation, intervention, and the Pygmalion effect', *Journal of Business Ethics* 128(1): 133–147.
Jenkins, M.R., A.L. Lewis & A.J. McKee (2015) 'Reflections at a rural university: Increasing critical thinking skills through cross-disciplinary access for education, nursing, criminal justice, and social work', *National Teacher Education Journal* 8(1): 47–52.
Jones, M.D. (2009) *The Thinker's Toolkit. Fourteen Powerful Techniques for Problem Solving*, New York: Three Rivers Press.
Kahneman, D. (2011) *Thinking Fast and Slow*, New York: Farrar, Straus and Giroux.
Kaller, M. (2014) *Think Smarter. Critical Thinking to Improve Problem-Solving and Decision-Making Skills*, Hoboken, NJ: John Wiley.
Krathwohl, D.R. (2002) 'A revision of Bloom's taxonomy: An overview', *Theory into Practice* 41(4): 212–218.
Lewine, R., A. Sommers, R. Waford & C. Robertson (2015) 'Setting the mood for critical thinking in the classroom', *International Journal for the Scholarship of Teaching & Learning* 9(2): 1–4.

Mitchell, S. (2006) 'Socratic dialogue, the humanities and the art of the question', *Arts & Humanities in Higher Education* 5(2): 181–197.

Moon, J.A. (2008) *Critical Thinking: An Exploration of Theory and Practice*, London: Routledge.

Nicholson-Preuss, M.L. (2013) *Social Sciences Student Engagement Strategies*, San Diego, CA: AVID Press.

Nosich, G.M. (2012) *Learning to Think Things Through: A Guide to Critical Thinking Across the Curriculum*, London: Prentice Hall.

Oyler, D.R. & F. Romanelli (2014) 'The fact of ignorance: Revisiting the Socratic method as a tool for teaching critical thinking', *American Journal of Pharmaceutical Education* 78(7): 1–9.

Smith, E. (2011) 'Teaching critical reflection', *Teaching in Higher Education* 16(2): 211–223.

Tredway, L. (1995) 'Socratic seminars: Engaging students in intellectual discourse', *Educational Leadership* 53(1): 26–29.

Wright, L. (2001) *Critical Thinking: An Introduction to Analytical Reading and Reasoning*, New York: Oxford University Press.

Zare, P. & J. Mukundan (2015) 'The use of Socratic method as a teaching/learning tool to develop students' critical thinking: A review of literature', *Language in India* 15(6): 256–265.

Conclusion

The higher education sectors in the United Kingdom, United States, Australia and New Zealand are all undergoing significant change which has been caused by, on the whole, international imperatives for a more educated, more highly skilled, general population. The argument is made that we need a working population equipped to meet the needs of modern economies no longer based on primary or secondary industry, but on technologies and 'knowledge' economies.

In order to bring this about, governments in all four countries manufactured national goals relating to the percentage of their populations they wished to possess an undergraduate degree. A corollary of such goals was the provision of university access to demographic groupings who did not traditionally attain a tertiary education. At varying times and places, these included women, Latinos, people from low socio-economic backgrounds, Māori, people from ethnically diverse backgrounds, Afro-Americans, Pasifika, and Indigenous Australians.

Government policy was attuned to these ambitions, and as a result, universities were requested (to varying extents) to participate in the massification, or widening participation, project. As discussed in chapter 1, the extent to which each university contributed to the project depended on their relative rank in the league tables, and ultimately, on their reputation for excellence. As a result, the universities admitting a higher proportion of first-in-family students tended to be those at the bottom, rather than at the top, of the league tables.

First-generation students entering universities commonly find themselves in a pressured situation: they have to balance their part-time employment demands; commonly they have to travel long distances to attend class; many have family and community commitments to meet; and, critically, they are required to learn the sometimes obscure behavioural protocols universities expect alongside a wide range of new academic literacies. Balancing these complex factors is extremely difficult and, as a consequence, many such students leave their course. Some return later, but many do not. So whilst the participation rates of first-generation students have increased, these are not commensurate with their graduation rates.

Why this is the case has been addressed in this book: students leave for a variety of social and familial factors over which universities have no control. But they also leave because their experiences at universities are not sufficiently affirming to persuade them to persist through a degree, and universities can act to improve this.

Of course all universities already have a wide range of student-facing support services such as counselling, health services, study support, sometimes financial support, housing support, social support, employment services and so forth which can intervene when the demand of social and familial factors becomes problematic. They can act as means of rescue when the issues confronting a first-generation (or any) student combine in a way which threatens their continuing enrolment.

But universities can also intervene through ensuring that their teaching staff are not only aware of the diverse learning needs of their incoming students, but fully equipped to meet them. This can be a challenge when teaching staff have no teaching qualifications, when there are increasingly high numbers of casual teaching staff who may have little or no knowledge of (or even commitment to) the university's learning and teaching culture and when teaching *per se* is viewed as a chore to be done prior to (or alongside) research which carries much more prestige in terms of a lifelong career.

The pedagogies discussed and outlined in this book are specifically designed to meet the needs of first-generation students – particularly in the first year of their degree – but work equally well with those from university-going backgrounds.

If these teaching strategies are used widely, universities become more cognate with diverse students, and the teaching staff who use them gain greater satisfaction from their pedagogical work.

Ultimately, despite the myriad pressures on staff and students alike, both are more highly engaged, and both achieve more.

Index

academic literacies 24, 36, 130
academics 11, 13, 23, 24, 29, 32, 36, 68, 82, 83
ACAPS (Author, Context, Audience, Purpose, Significance) 72, 78, 85, 100–1
access to university 1, 6, 9–11, 21, 36, 130
active learning 45, 93, 110
Analysing Artefacts 79
Analysing Graphs 79–80
Analysing Photographs 77–8
Analysing Questions 75–7
Analysing Sound Recordings 81, 83
Analysing Structure 73–4
analysis 13, 30, 77–86, 99, 117, 118, 126
Approaching Writing Tasks 74–5
Archer, Louise 4, 6, 7, 12, 23, 86
aspiration 2, 4–7, 21, 23, 24, 35
Assessing Academic Credibility 81–4
assessment practices 8, 67
assessment tasks 43, 51, 74, 77, 83
attrition 9, 21, 36, 44, 68, 93
Australia 1, 2, 3, 5, 6, 7, 10, 13, 19, 20, 22, 23, 26, 32, 109, 133

Black rights movement 3
Black students 3, 7, 22
Bloom's revised taxonomy 74, 117–19
Bourdieu, Louis 6, 11, 19, 21

casual staff 12, 23, 24, 25, 30, 134
civic engagement 3, 20, 32
classroom 11, 12, 13, 22, 23, 24, 27, 30, 31, 33, 36, 45, 53, 55, 63, 68, 69, 93, 95, 96, 98, 107, 109, 110, 117, 118

classroom culture 23, 27, 36, 45, 46, 53, 63, 93, 96, 98
cognition 115, 117, 118, 119, 121, 126, 130
collaborative learning 23, 24, 36, 44, 45, 53, 64, 94, 95, 98, 100, 101, 106, 107, 109, 110, 113, 119, 122, 125, 130
commitment 29, 31, 44, 56, 63, 94, 97, 114, 113, 134
communication skills 43, 44, 84, 94
confidence 8, 31, 34, 36, 43, 50, 58, 60, 62, 69, 79, 80, 84, 85, 86, 101, 108, 109, 123
confusion 33, 59, 120
connaissance 12, 13, 23
cooperative learning 93, 96, 98
credibility 73, 81–4, 96, 114, 130
critical education 11, 113, 117
critical thinking 21, 23, 24, 31, 36, 53, 64, 69, 70, 71, 84, 95, 100, 101, 105, 106, 108, 110, 113–32
cultural capital 8, 21, 130
curriculum 9, 22, 30, 47, 55, 109

data 2, 24, 29, 32, 36, 51, 72, 79–80, 82, 83, 86, 106, 110, 124, 128
Data Processing 51–2
democracy 4, 10, 19
demographic cohorts 3–5
developing oral fluency 84, 86
Dewey 113–14, 130
dialogic 45, 58, 63, 85, 98
disadvantage 5, 7, 10, 44, 76, 118
disciplines 23, 43, 81, 115, 121
discourse xiii, 4–6, 9–11, 68
discussion protocols 86, 94–5, 101–2, 105

disruption 114, 123
diversity 1, 3, 4, 5, 6, 21, 68

educational capital 8, 21, 68, 130
egalitarian xiv, 7, 27
elite 2–3, 6–7
empathy 24, 32, 56, 59
employment 4, 6, 10, 12, 25, 133, 134
engagement xiv, 1, 3, 11, 19, 24, 27, 28, 29–35, 45, 46, 63, 71, 73, 94, 96, 97, 99, 102–3, 122, 124
enjoyment 25–6, 35
enquiry 26, 44, 53, 76, 79, 83, 100, 108, 118
entrance requirements 6, 10
equality 27
Essential Question 115–16, 118
ethnicity 19
ethnic minority 3, 22
evaluation 10, 12, 24, 36, 77, 108, 109, 117, 118, 125
evidence 10, 29, 35, 73, 74, 77, 83, 85, 86, 94, 95, 96, 102, 103, 110, 113, 114, 115, 116, 118, 123, 125, 126
experience 1, 4, 21, 22, 24, 27, 28, 31, 33, 50, 52, 53, 57, 59, 60–3, 110, 123, 134
Expert Jigsaw 72, 81, 85, 98, 99–100, 101
explicit 23, 24, 28, 30, 36, 46, 50, 52, 53, 54, 61, 68, 69, 84, 86, 93, 94, 96, 97, 101, 102, 105, 113, 114, 119, 120, 123, 128, 130

first-generation students 1, 27, 33, 134
first-in-family 1, 8, 22, 24, 27, 50, 60, 134
first year experience 22, 134
flexible learning 30, 43, 44, 67
Folded Line, The 58
formative assessment 8, 43, 74, 121, 128
Foucault, Michel 12–13, 23, 27
Frayer Model, The 121–3, 127
free market 2–3, 7, 10, 12
Freire, Paulo 1, 13, 113

government 1–5, 10, 19, 21, 44, 80, 110, 133
grades xiv, 30
graduate attributes 43–4, 110
graduates 3, 20, 32, 43, 44, 110, 113, 130
graduation rates 3, 20–1, 133
Graphic Organisers 126–130

habits of mind 43, 84, 102, 110
habitus 6, 22, 86
hidden curriculum 9
hierarchy 117, 127, 130
higher education xiv, 1–13, 21–4, 32, 36, 43, 44, 60, 67–8, 72, 81, 84, 109–10, 133
higher order thinking xiv, 97, 114–16, 123, 130
human capital 4, 11

Indigenous Australian 22, 133
international 1–2, 5–7, 9, 20, 21, 30

Jigsaw 98–9

knowledge 1, 4, 8–11, 13, 26, 27, 28, 43, 57, 67, 69, 71, 79, 82, 99, 100, 101, 106, 107, 109, 110, 113, 116–18, 121, 122, 127, 134
knowledge economies 133

Latino 3, 7, 22, 133
league tables 1, 3, 6, 7, 9, 12, 23, 133
learning outcomes 31, 93, 94, 110
learning styles 43, 67, 74
Learning the Language I 69–70
Learning the Language II 70
Learning the Language III 70–1
lecturers 21, 22, 34
lifelong learning 26, 60, 71, 110
low-socioeconomic background 8, 19

Māori 3, 22, 133
Marking the Text 72, 73
massification 1–6, 9–10, 68, 133
Meditation 61–2
metacognition 115, 118, 123, 126, 130
middle class 3, 36
modelling 24, 34
motivation 24, 32, 79
Mystery Classmate 49

Name Tents 46–7
neoliberalism 6, 10, 12–13
New Zealand xiii, 1, 2, 3, 5, 6, 7, 10, 13, 19, 20, 26, 32, 109, 133

OECD 1, 2, 5, 110
online learning 8, 36, 43, 44, 68, 74, 77, 81, 82, 83, 109, 126

participation rate 1, 3, 4, 6, 8, 9, 11–13, 20–1, 26, 109, 133
partnership 6, 10, 25, 70, 96
Pasifika 3, 22, 133
pedagogical cultures 36, 46, 67
Pedagogical Work 11–13, 19, 23–7, 32, 35, 36, 134
People Bingo 47–9, 50
persistence xiv, 33, 34, 63, 114
Philosophical Chairs 86, 106, 123–6
plagiarism 43, 68
policy 1–5, 20–1, 32, 110, 133
Position Line 106
power 5, 10, 11, 13, 23, 24, 27–32, 35, 53, 59, 61, 77, 100, 109, 119
pre-reading 69, 71, 86
prior knowledge 69, 71, 79, 100, 107, 110, 121, 127
problem solving 58, 96, 113
protocols xiv, 1, 8, 9, 22, 36, 52, 54, 68, 85–7, 94–5, 101–2, 105, 125, 134

Questioning Levels 101, 116–21
questions 4, 27, 28, 46, 53, 56–7, 61, 74–5, 78–81, 83, 85–6, 97, 101–2, 107, 109, 113, 114, 116–20

rankings 7, 9
reading 49, 68–73, 80, 98–9, 123
reasoning 6, 11, 48, 71, 72, 84, 98, 106, 115, 116
relationships 10, 12, 22, 24, 27, 29, 35, 53, 93, 101, 127
research xiii, 7, 8, 9, 12, 20, 24, 30, 74, 82, 83, 86, 100, 101, 104, 105, 110, 134
retention 21, 24, 27, 30, 31, 45, 63, 94

savoir 12, 13, 23, 27
scaffolding xiv, 44, 46, 58, 69, 71, 72, 79, 94, 99, 123
scholarly xiv, 69, 82, 114, 115, 123
School Days 60–1
schools 4, 6, 10, 21, 34, 36, 60–1, 98, 110, 115, 121
secondary education 36, 60, 62, 95, 101, 110, 117
self-awareness 60, 115, 116, 119, 123, 130
sex 19, 24, 54

Shoe Mountain 50
Six Word Memoir, The 59–60
skills 1, 8, 9, 30, 31, 43, 44, 59, 64, 67, 68, 69, 71, 79, 84, 87, 94, 95, 97, 101, 105, 106, 110, 113, 114, 115, 116, 123, 124, 130
social capital xiv, 8, 36
social cohesion 3
Social Contract 53–5, 94, 97
social inclusion 1, 4, 5, 6, 9, 10, 13, 23, 130
social inequality 6
social justice 4
social mobility 10
Socratic Seminar 72, 85, 86, 94, 95, 101–5, 106, 118, 123
Speakers' Panel 85–6
Standing Order 52
student-centred learning 23, 30, 45
student evaluations 12, 24, 36, 108, 109
study skills 9, 30, 31, 68, 87
subjectivity 13, 24
success xiii, 7, 11, 23, 24, 30, 31, 36, 50, 58, 63, 69, 71, 84, 86, 93, 95, 103
support 22, 33, 34, 44, 68, 84, 85, 99, 115, 116, 130, 134
synthesis 115, 117, 118

teaching moment 23, 25, 64, 79, 80
Team Building 97–8
teamwork 42, 51, 54, 67, 94
tertiary education 1–9, 19–20, 36, 60, 61, 62, 84, 95, 110, 115, 117, 133
Things Done Well 62–3
Think-Pair-Share 95–6
time poverty 44
transformation 12, 13, 21, 32, 35
transition 6, 21, 22, 29, 33, 60
transparent pedagogies xiii, 1, 13, 19, 22–4, 26–32, 35, 36, 70, 86, 96
tutorials 8, 27, 44, 69, 78, 116
tutors 21, 22, 25, 53, 69, 80
Two-Minute Speeches 84–5

undergraduates xiii, xiv, 2, 7, 8, 20, 24, 36, 79, 82, 83, 84, 133
understanding xiv, 8, 13, 23, 27, 31, 33, 35, 43, 53, 55, 58, 61, 67, 69, 73, 74, 75, 86, 98, 99, 101, 102, 103, 106, 109, 114–21, 126, 130

United Kingdom xiii, 1, 2, 3, 5, 6, 7, 10, 11, 13, 19, 20, 22, 26, 32, 109, 133
United States xiii, 1, 2, 3, 5, 6, 7, 13, 19, 20, 22, 26, 32, 109, 133
Unpacking the Text 73
Unusual Questions 57
Using Imagery 55–6

viewpoints 114, 123, 130

Weird Connections 50–1, 97
widening participation 1, 6, 11, 12, 13, 20, 21, 26, 133
workforce 3, 25, 30, 43, 67
workload 11, 25, 108
workplace 94, 110, 130
World Café, The 106–9

Zap the Problem 58, 96–7

For Product Safety Concerns and Information please contact our EU
representative GPSR@taylorandfrancis.com
Taylor & Francis Verlag GmbH, Kaufingerstraße 24, 80331 München, Germany

www.ingramcontent.com/pod-product-compliance
Lightning Source LLC
Chambersburg PA
CBHW051615230426
43668CB00013B/2115